A Vegetarians ecstasy

A Healthy Gourmet Celebration of over 250 no cholesterol, no dairy, lowfat recipes devoted to long life and good taste

Natalie Cederquist and James Levin, M.D.

Illustrations by
Natalie Cederquist

Published by
Hummingbird Graphics

First Edition
Revised Version

Published by

Hummingbird GRAPHICS

Worldwide distribution by GLO, Inc.

For information address:
GLO, Inc., 2406 Fifth Avenue, San Diego, CA 92101
U.S.A. and Canada call 1-800-854-2587 toll free
All other countries call 1-619-233-9165

Printed and bound in U.S.A.

Library of Congress Catalog Card Number 90-86040
ISBN 0-9628698-0-5

Typesetting by TypeGraphics

This cookbook is dedicated to the ultimate health of all people. We inhabit this divine body, it is a gift, so please take care of it and of each other. Eating fresh, wholesome, light and alive foods will fill you full of their vitality and enable you to feel better than ever before. As each cell dances in celebration of the Universal vibration, you too will radiate this inner clarity of love.

Table of Contents

Foreword

A *Vegetarians Ecstasy* is a book for everyone, designed to show us how a high fiber, fresh fruit and vegetable diet with minimal fat can be divinely delicious.

The recipes herein include those from the exotic Pacific Rim to the sensual soulfood of Mexico and South America. Each recipe has easy to read large type and instructions for simple step by step preparation. The magical and inspired illustrations found throughout this book awaken ones visual appetite as well.

Most cookbooks (even vegetarian) call for too much fat, in the form of butter, dairy products, eggs, and other animal products.

We don't need all that fat!

I have spent several years improvising and substituting fresh herbs, lemon juice, wines, soy products, tamari and vegetable broth to create a low fat tasty cuisine that is health promoting. We can sauté without butter or oil and still have our food taste great.

For the health and survival of our planet Earth and for our own personal health, it is time to learn a new way of eating; one that is environmentally clean and efficient, utilizing the dynamic variety of fresh produce, grains, beans, herbs and spices available.

This new way of eating is *A Vegetarians Ecstasy!*

Introduction

A special feast awaits you inside *A Vegetarians Ecstasy*. Over 250 healthful recipes have been prepared dedicated to long life and good taste.

My vision is to present an ethnic variety of light sauces, salads, main dishes and desserts that elevate you into higher culinary consciousness.

Going beyond mere recipes I hope to encourage you towards the foods that give you more energy and vitality. The phrase "you are what you eat" is true on many levels, for health isn't just a diet but a way of life affected by what we eat, our state of mind, and our relationships. Real health involves the whole person, body, mind and soul.

Whole natural food brings to us a greater radiance and inner health. We consume the ultimate nutrition and energy when we eat raw and sprouted foods. Cooking destroys many of the vitamins and minerals of vegetables and fruits, so if possible, have a raw salad and plenty of fresh fruit everyday. Begin substituting whole grains (wheat berries, brown rice, etc.) for refined flour products (breads, muffins, pastry). Whole grains provide the roughage and nutrition you need, balance your blood sugar levels, and usually contain less fat.

It takes more than healthy eating to maintain optimum health, for in addition health is also a state of mind. Our mental pictures are the videotape for our physical well being. Visualize health, love, joy, peace, success and beauty and you will attract those things in your life. You are God's creation, what you create in your life is your gift in return.

By exercising and expending energy, you will gain energy. That is why a daily physical workout (whether walking, biking, swimming or dancing) is important for increasing your vitality and vigor, and will keep you looking and feeling younger. Also, surround yourself with positive people. The more loving, supportive, and harmonious our environment, the more conducive it is to experiencing a fuller healthier life.

I see food not only as nourishment, but as a celebration of life. Be thankful for what you have, let love flow into your meal preparation and remember, real flavor comes from the heart.

May this book inspire your
journey into lighter healthier eating.

Enjoy,
Natalie Cederquist
James Levin, M.D.

Buy Organic!

Did you know that the cell of an organically grown fruit or vegetable has a more vibrant and radiant life force than one smothered in chemical fertilizers and pesticides? One can certainly taste the difference. The organic one is tastier, sweeter and more potent than the commercial variety.

As we read about the ill effects pesticides have on our bodies, why take a chance?

Discover where to find organic produce in your area. By making the choice to shop organic you are supporting the organic farmers, and creating demand for a pesticide-free farm industry, which will lower the prices for organic produce thru supply and demand. You will also consume a more nutritious product, rather than one depleted of its vitamins, minerals and trace elements from the leeching of toxic chemicals.

Growing your own seasonal vegetables and herbs is worth the effort. Try planting tomatoes in a 5 gallon tub, or herbs in a window box. One prolific zucchini plant should yield a summer supply of tender zucchinis. Planting also has a positive effect on our well-being.

If you can't buy organic then scrub or peel the produce or soak it in a vinegar bath several minutes before preparation.

Just add 1 tbl. of white vinegar to a sinkful of cool filtered water, it will help rinse away some of the toxic residues.

And always send love into your meal by being thankful for what you are given.

Fats & Oils

Why not to heat them

Fatty acids, the building blocks of the fats in human bodies are a major energy source and important for the maintenance and construction of healthy cells. **Essential Fatty Acids** are called "essential" because our body doesn't manufacture them. Fresh raw seeds (especially flax seeds, see "Healing Heroes!"), nuts and oils are the healthiest sources of these fatty acids. When these natural and easily absorbed oils are heated above 320°F (160°c), their molecular structure transforms becoming harmful to our system, causing cellular degeneration.[1]

The process of hydrogenation turns liquid oil into hardened oil (shortenings and margarines) which destroys the Essential Fatty Acids (EFA's).

These adultered fats don't belong in our bodies precise architectural plan. They become blocks to the natural life energy flow from cell to cell and impede the body's ability to absorb EFA's. They also may encourage blood clots, fatty deposits in the liver (and other organs) and arteries. Fatty deposits in the arteries may lead to atherosclerosis. When our arteries are blocked the oxygen and blood can't flow to the heart and brain, so strokes and heart attacks are more likely to occur unless we clean up our diet.

For your health, it is best to avoid all products with hydrogenated and partially hydrogenated ingredients—read labels! In addition to margarine and shortening hydrogenated products may be found in bakery goods, chips, crackers, fried foods and cereals. Some countries like Holland have banned the sale of margarines containing the altered fatty acids, interestingly, the Dutch are reported to have an average life expectancy 5 years longer than in the U.S.[2]

Oxidation and light also destroy the EFA's, therefore purchase oil in dark or metal containers, when possible.

Use only fresh, organic, mechanically pressed oil. Some good oils are walnut, safflower, olive, sesame, almond and flax (if you can find it). Avoid cottonseed oil, it is the most refined and pesticide contaminated oil.

Traditional frying overheats the oil (428°F), so take the care to use oil safely by *adding water to the pan first*. In traditional chinese cooking the water is put into a very hot wok, *then* the oil is added. The water will hold the temperature under 212°F, safe for the EFA's, and the waters vapor will guard against oxidation.

I prefer to use the sensitive oils, raw and uncooked for the most benefit in salad dressings or in the liver flush. For healthful cooking use lemon juice, sake or wine, aminos and tamari to sauté your foods in. If desired, use a special oil, (like toasted sesame oil) after cooking has been done.

You will preserve more than just the flavor, you will preserve your health.

How to Sauté without Oil

Heat 2-3 Tbl. of water or vegetable broth in a heavy skillet. Add a bit of liquid aminos or tamari if you wish, and a splash of lemon juice, quality wine, sake or combination thereof. To enhance the taste of your vegetables, add your choice of the aromatics: minced ginger, garlic, onions, chile peppers or fresh herbs, and sauté on low a couple of minutes. Next, place in your chopped veggies, stirring well to coat, sauté either covered or uncovered until al dente; season as desired. Cooking time depends on the size and quantity of the vegetables.

If you do decide to use oil in your sauté, add water to the pan first. The vapor will protect the oil from the heat, you'll use less fat, and you'll enjoy a healthier product.

Glossary of Ingredients

Here is a guide to frequently used ingredients that might seem rather unusual at first. You can find all these foods in natural food stores or co-ops. These are vegetarian alternatives, supplements and staples. Stock and use these healthier substitutes instead of salt, cornstarch, eggs and meat, etc.

Agar Agar
A seaweed based thickener that gives a gelatinous body to foods. Especially good in fruit gels.

Arrowroot Powder
An herbal thickener, that when mixed with water into a paste thickens sauces and gravies; use instead of flour or cornstarch. Cornstarch creates a pasty glue-like coating over your intestines, and should be avoided.

Brewers and Nutritional Yeast
A potent vitamin, mineral, amino acid nutritive yeast that can be added to anything. It is one of the best sources of vitamin B-12. Add 1 TBL daily to supplement your foods. Put it in your morning smoothies or atop a salad.

Egg Replacer
A potato starch and tapioca based flour, a leaven and binder that substitutes for egg yolks and whites. Use 1 1/2 tsp. mixed with 2 Tbl water to replace 1 egg. One can also try tofu mashed with water as an egg replacer.

Liquid Aminos
A mineral rich soy bouillon developed by health pioneer Paul Bragg. It is a salt substitute with a distinctive delicious flavor to be used in sauces, dressings, salads, stir-frys and over vegetables. Use in a sauté along with water instead of oil and butter.

Mirin Cooking Sake

Mirin is the name of cooking sake. Sake is made from the action of a yeast-like mold on rice. It tenderizes and enhances your sautés and sauces, imparting natural sweetness.

Mirin has less alcohol than regular drinking sake. Look for it in Asian markets, or in the Oriental section of grocery stores.

Miso

An aged and fermented soy bean paste, high in B vitamins and enzymes. Thin with water, then add to soups and sauces during the last phase of cooking to keep all nutrients alive. Miso provides a nice flavor and adds body to soups, sauces and gravies.

Seitan

A wheat gluten product that is found in the refrigerated section in natural food stores. Formed into a ball, seitan marinates in a savory sauce. You can slice it thin or cube it, marinate with spices or barbeque it. Seitan was developed by Japanese warrior monks. It has a good meaty texture, and is high in protein and keeps in the refrigerator if well covered.

Seaweeds

Raised and bathed in the ocean, sea vegetables are charged with minerals, iodine, vitamins D, E, K, and B-complex, calcium and magnesium. They are healing to mucous membranes, skin irritations, colds, constipation and arthritis. There are many varieties: nori, wakame, hijiki, dulse, kombu. Rinse well several times before using, and add to salads or use as a condiment. Nutritious sea vegetables are a superior food, being so prolific they can be harvested daily to feed this malnourished planet of ours.

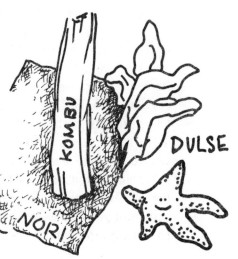

HIJIKI

Tahini

Tahini has been used for over 3,000 years by the Egyptians and other cultures in the Middle East. This slightly bitter sesame butter thickens sauces, dressings and dips and is a great complement to rice and tofu. Mix with honey, bee pollen and dried fruit to create natural candies. Tahini is a good replacement for rich butter or dairy products.

Tamari

A naturally fermented soy bean sauce. Tamari is more concentrated than soy sauce, for soy sauce is created from wheat and is a bit milder. Also, soy sauce usually contains sugar or preservatives, so be sure to search out the naturally brewed kind. Remember to dilute tamari with water when using recipes calling for "soy sauce".

Tempeh

A staple and complete protein native to Indonesia. Soy beans are cooked, pressed into cakes and fermented. Steam, cook or marinate first, then enjoy with a myriad of sauces. Baked, broiled or barbequed, tempeh is a delicious meaty substitute high in B-12 and cholesterol free.

Tofu

Pressed soybean curd is lowfat, containing no cholesterol, and is a truly versatile high protein food. Its use is endless, from dips and drinks to main dishes and desserts. It comes in many varieties: soft, firm, silken and regular. Use the firm in stirfrys, and reserve the silken for blended sauces and desserts. Tofu has a neutral taste and it takes on whatever spice or seasoning you use with it. In summer months try serving it chilled and cubed in a bowl. Serve with separate seasonings such as minced green onions, tamari, ginger, and toasted sesame seeds.

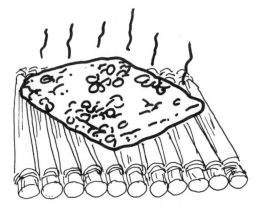

Exotic Mushrooms

There are several types of edible fungi (mushrooms) that are nutritious and considered a delicacy. Substitute them for white cap mushrooms to add variety and a new taste sensation.

All fresh mushrooms are wonderful in salads or stirfrys, and are preferred over canned varieties.

Enoki mushrooms are long, delicate and slender, resembling a sprout with a creamy colored small cap, use them whole.

Oyster mushrooms are large and flat, disc shaped and delicious.

Shiitake mushrooms are a large capped meaty mushroom, the thicker the better, great fresh or dried. Soak dried ones in warm water 20 minutes before stemming and adding to the wok.

Woodears are a rubbery fungus that have long been known in the East as a blood thinner. This beneficial anticoagulant keeps sticky platelets free flowing, here in the West we are just discovering its terrific qualities. Woodears yield little taste, but they add a lot of texture in woked dishes or salads.

Japanese Horseradish (Wasabi Powder)

Reconstitute wasabi in a small cup, mixing in a few drops of hot water to make a thick green paste. Its sharp flavor will ripen as it sits a few minutes; make only what you'll use for it will not keep. Its hot "bite" will clear your nasal passages effectively, and spice up sauces. Traditionally mixed with soy sauce to make a dipping sauce for sushi.

Enoki mushrooms

shiitake mushrooms

Dried Woodears

JAPANESE HORSE RADISH

Healing Heroes!

All raw fruits and vegetables are healing and nutritious, but there are those that are extraordinary. Here are a few of my favorites.

Have these wonder foods in stock at all times to cleanse, heal and protect your system against infection and environmental pollutants. Incorporate them into your daily regime for long life and good taste.

Garlic

Garlic is truly a blessed bulb, much revered for centuries for its medicinal properties. Its use in the remedy of 22 ailments was recorded in an Egyptian Medical listing, dated 1550 B.C. Garlic's healing qualities are also mentioned in a calendar of the Hsai dated 2000 B.C.[3]

Its anti-bacterial action is akin to penicillin and it has been used to treat high blood pressure, cardiac and circulatory problems, a wash for wounds and ulcers, a cure for worms and parasites, for reducing cholesterol and preventing gastric cancer.

It eats away the skin (lipid layer) of harmful bacteria, preventing them from breathing, thus destroying them. Its healing power is released when the clove is crushed, evident by its powerful odor. Its beneficial properties are unstable in heat, so use garlic raw as much as possible. To retain the healing properties and fullest flavor, try stirring in pressed garlic after the sauce has finished cooking.

For an easy way to peel a clove of garlic, hit the top with the flat side of a knife, or with the bottom of a mug. This will loosen the outer skin making it easy to peel off before chopping or pressing the garlic clove.

Ginger

This wondrous aromatic rhizome is soothing to the digestive system, stimulating to the circulary system, dispels gas, and works as a decongestant. It has been honored in ancient India and China and truly has an exotic taste.

Use it raw in dressings, soups, sauces, and breads. As a tea, pour boiling water over chopped ginger for a warming effect when feeling chilled. Ginger is used in the Orange Flush.*

Lemon

A fantastic cleanser! It aids digestion, decongests, cleanses and stimulates the liver, it is a tonic to the heart and stomach and purifies the blood stream.

For extra strengthening to the liver add grated lemon peel to your raw salad. Each morning on an empty stomach take 1/2 lemon juiced in warm water to cleanse your system and rid yourself of excess mucus—a great way to begin your day.

Flax

Its name derived from Latin means *most useful* and that it is. One of the oldest cultivated plants in history, flax is not only nutritious, but it is believed to be helpful in preventing disease and infection.

Flax has been of service to humanity prior to recorded history. Flax seeds and fiber cloth (linen) were found in archeological digs of ancient Babylonia, Egyptian burial chambers and Europe's stoneage ancestors, dating as far back as 5,000 B.C.

*See page 34.

The oil in flax seed is the richest source of the Essential Fatty Acids LNA (linolenic acid) and LA (linoleic acid). "Essential" because the body cannot produce them. They are necessary for healthy nerves, arteries and blood. Flax regulates blood pressure and aids in the digestion and elimination of toxins due to its high mucilage and fiber content. It is a complete and easily digested protein, as well as an excellent vitamin and mineral source.

Good fresh Flax oil, due to its 3-month shelf life and extreme sensitivity to light, is seldom seen in the health food stores.

To add Flax to your diet, try grinding it fresh minutes before use, or try the gomasio listed in the condiment section. Use it on salads, in your cereal, casseroles and smoothies, or just chew on a few seeds throughout the day.

Carrots

Carrots are good for increasing vitality, and the fresh raw juice is good for normalizing the entire system. Carrots aid in digestion, help to build blood, improve and maintain the bone structure and have been known to heal and prevent eye, throat, sinus and respiratory infections. Carrots are high in beta carotene (which helps the liver to isolate vitamin A).

Carrot juice is the richest source of vitamin

A that the body can quickly assimilate. Fresh carrot juice also contains ample amounts of vitamins B, C, D, E, G and K.[4]

Carrot juice helps the liver to eliminate toxins via the lymph system and skin pores, thus if your skin turns an orange-like color it is due to this internal cleansing and is not caused from the orange color (or carotene) of carrot juice. Otherwise we would turn red from beets or turn green from broccoli. It is a great sign to know we are getting toxins out of us. Live raw juices are truly terrific builders of health, they contain many enzymes and nutrients. If you are in need of a cleansing, fresh carrot juice may be used in a purifying fast.

Sprouts

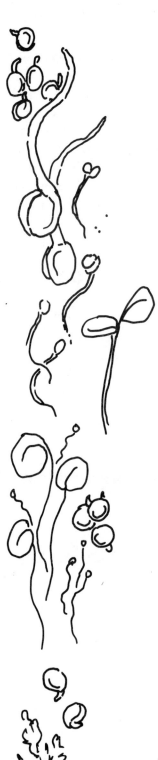

The most alive foods on Earth are sprouts, for they are still growing at the table. Their protein, vitamin and mineral content rivals and surpasses almost any food. Sprouts are *biogenic*, full of vital life forces which build, cleanse, repair and strengthen our cells.

Awaken this life force by soaking the seeds or beans overnight in a glass jar filled with water. This soaking activates the enzymes in the sprouts which convert their starches into simple sugars, changes their complex fats into useable carbohydrates, and balances and predigests their proteins into an easily assimilated low calorie food source for just pennies.

The moisture content of sprouts also increases from about 10% to 88%, which is compositionally similar to any fruit, and to our own bodies.

Sprouts can be grown anywhere, anytime in just 3-7 days, they are your indoor organic garden.

Try sprouting lentils, alfalfa or mung beans to start, they are the easiest to sprout.

Simple Sprouting
1) Use 1/4c lentils, or mung beans, or 2 Tbl. alfalfa seeds per quart size glass jar.
2) Cover with pure water for 8-12 hours.
3) Rinse and drain 2 times daily (morning and night)
4) Put in sunlight for greenery to appear. Use either a screen or cheesecloth as a strainer for the top of the jar.

Beet & Carrot Greens
Create tender gourmet greens for your salads by placing the tops of these roots in a shallow pan of water for a few days. Cut off greens as they grow.

Other Power Foods

Ginseng

The ancient Chinese health tonic for long life and enhanced physical performance is ginseng. The root is now harvested in the U.S. and is available in capsules, concentrates, teas and soft drinks. I enjoy it in liquid form added to juices and teas. In China they prescribe it for everything, especially for male vitality and increased energy.

Bee Pollen, Royal Jelly and Propolis

Pollen is one of the richest sources of vitamins, minerals, enzymes, fats, hormones, protein and amino acids. It has restorative properties for the entire system. One to three teaspoons is said to improve health, athletic performance and physical endurance. It is one of natures precious power foods, resembling multi-colored golden nuggets. Bee pollen has been used for many medical problems such as anaemia, colon disorders and allergies.

Royal bee jelly is secreted by the Queen Bee to feed other potential Royal Queen Bees. It is high in B vitamins and pantothenic acid, a cellular rejuvenator and energy-enhancer, it is also an excellent tonic for the heart.

The resinous substance gathered by the bees that is used to maintain and disinfect their hives is propolis. It is high in B complex vitamins and amino acids. Its natural antibiotic effect is said to heal wounds, ulcers, sore throats, oral infections and coughs. Look for the propolis lozenges and cough syrups now available in health food stores.

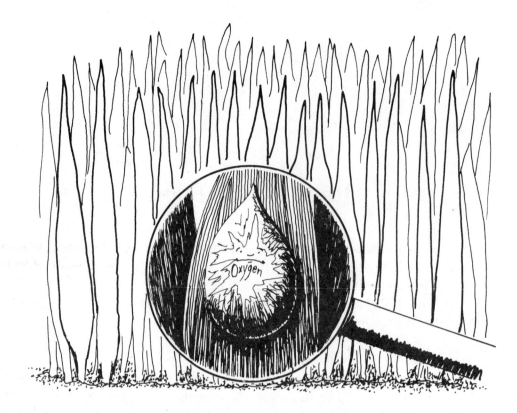

Wheatgrass Juice

Imagine drinking concentrated emeralds, liquid sweet and potent, healing and rejuvenating every cell of your body . . . welcome to wheatgrass juice! It is a complete food that detoxifies as it nourishes. Dr. G. H. Earp-Thomas, scientist and soil expert, has isolated over 100 elements and all the known minerals contained in wheatgrass. It contains almost the identical molecular makeup as the hemoglobin molecule of human blood, the difference is magnesium instead of iron. It oxygenates your system and it helps to build blood cells. It is said to produce an immunization effect against carcinogens, and to offset the effects of smog and environmental pollutants, x-rays and radiation. Truly this is a wonder food! If you don't grow wheatgrass, or have a juicer for that purpose, then call around to your local health food stores or juice bars to find out where you can get it freshly pressed. One ounce daily is sufficient, you can dilute it with water or fresh vegetable juice if desired. It is a healing wash for skin disorders and may be diluted for eye washes. Wheatgrass juice is such a powerful cleanser that you might have a few discomforts at first, but with continued usage it will detoxify your body and strengthen your entire system. Other chlorophyll rich supplements worth trying are bluegreen algae, spirulina and barley grass juice, they all share similar astounding health building properties.

Chiles

Chiles are a passion in the heart of Mexican and Indian cuisines. They are also gaining respect as a versatile vegetable and seasoning in nouvelle cooking. Chiles are loaded with vitamin C, high in iron, potassium and niacin. The niacin in chiles improves circulation, reduces cholesterol levels in the blood, and is said to protect cells against cancer.

Chiles are an effective guard against colds. They are fantastic stuffed, baked, roasted, minced or raw, and the hot ones are indispensable in salsas.

There are many kinds of peppers in the Chile (capsicum) family, here is a brief description of the most common ones.

Ancho or pasilla chiles

These chiles are rather heart shaped and are not as hot as the anaheim. The dried version is quite dark and wrinkly. The pulp is a classic for enchilada sauces, yielding a sweet and roasted flavor. Note: if the cooked pulp is black or dark brown it will make the sauce rather smokey flavored and bitter tasting.

Bell Peppers

The most familiar and versatile chiles are green peppers. When allowed to ripen on the vine they turn yellow then red, increasing in sweetness and nutrition.

California (anaheim) Chiles

Longer, thinner and hotter than the bell pepper, the anaheim chile can be roasted and peeled, stuffed and baked, or minced raw before adding to soups, sauces or main dishes.

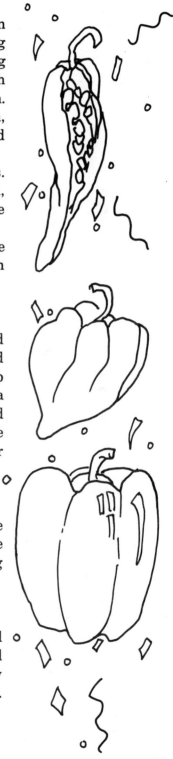

The seeds are hot, as with all chiles so discard before use or use with caution. As these chiles dry to a brick red color they become hotter. The cooked pulp is a natural thickener and adds an authentic flavor to sauces. Hanging chile clusters in your kitchen enables you to pull one off when you need one and adds a colorful ethnic adornment.

Jalapeños

Plump green peppers about 2'' in length. Raw, minced, sliced or roasted they are excellent in many sauce or main dish creations. They are hotter than the Ancho chiles.

Serranos

A small slender hot green pepper that can really spice up a soup or sauce. Frequently found floating in Thai soups for flavor, they are meant to be strained out. These can really make your eyes water, so be careful.

Cayenne Pepper

A favorite seasoning. Gives an invigorating warming effect by increasing circulation, which is beneficial to the heart and the blood stream. Try it in water with lemon juice as a daily tonic.

How to Roast a Chile

1) Preheat oven 450°
2) Rinse chile, blot dry, put on top rack of oven.
3) Turn chiles after a few minutes so the skin blisters evenly.
4) Pull out and put into a plastic bag until cool, or rinse in cool water peeling off skin, dig out seeds, keep stem on only if stuffing them.
5) Chop and add to your creations, or keep whole to make *Chiles Rellenos,* or other stuffed *exóticas*.

How to Handle a Chile

Wear rubber gloves! Or, wash your hands with soap and water before touching *anything* else.

Let's hear it for the bean....

Soy Products

Dairyless and Eggless
With optimum health in mind, I have chosen to use soy products and egg replacer rather than dairy and eggs. Dairy is mucus forming, it contains cholesterol, fat and hormones, in addition to the pesticides and antibiotics used in the farming and dairy industry.

Soy and seed cheeses, soy yogurts, soy cream cheese, soy sour cream, soy and rice based ice creams are delicious non-dairy products in the natural markets for you to try which are cholesterol free and low in fat.

BEGINNINGS
Introduction 31

HEALTHY BEGINNINGS
Breakfast Ecstasies

Upon arising, it is beneficial to awaken your system with warm water and lemon juice. This drink purifies your system (especially the liver) and flushes out impurities.

Follow this cleansing with the Orange Flush, then have herbal tea, or fresh juice of choice. I find that exercise is fantastic at this point, before eating solid foods. It will help you to wake up your system by flooding oxygen into your blood stream, circulating energy throughout your body and preparing you for a healthy assimilation of food. Have a good aerobic workout (minimum of 20 minutes) before breakfast.

The best break-fast I know is a bowl of fresh cut fruit. For a nourishing light meal make a fruit smoothie, they fill you up, are easy to digest, and are low in fat and calories. Try adding fresh or frozen fruit, soy-based protein powder, bee pollen, brewers yeast, tofu, bran or spirulina to fresh juice for a delicious meal. Complement it with a muffin for a super morning filler. You can make these muffins in advance, freeze them, and reheat in an oven when you want.

Any cooked whole grain makes a nourishing first meal, too. Try whole oats, rye flakes or müesli. Special brunch dishes like Tofu Rancheros, Tofu Florentine or Tofu Chilaquiles create celebrative weekend meals without oil, dairy or eggs.

Lemon Water

The morning cleanser

Begin your day with a cup of warm water with 1/2 a lemon juiced into it. You can also substitute 1/2 tsp of raw apple cider vinegar. This restores the acidic balance in your body, and is a very cleansing and purifying way to start your day.

Lemon juice flushes out impurities and excess mucus, cleans the liver and acts as a natural appetite supressant. Wait 15 to 30 minutes before consuming other beverages or foods, so the lemon has a chance to do its magic.

THE Orange Flush

This Liver flush was designed by Dr. Stone and has super cleansing, strengthening and invigorating properties for your liver and whole system in general. You can moderate the garlic and cayenne according to taste. The Purifying Diet by Dr. Stone is a wonderfully gentle way to heal and cleanse. It consists of this flush every morning and eating *only* fruits and vegetables, (raw or steamed) plus herbal teas throughout the day.

2 c Fresh squeezed orange/grapefruit juice
1/2 lemon juiced
1 tsp olive oil—extra virgin pure
1 tsp chopped fresh ginger
1 garlic clove
dash of cayenne

• Blend everything in blender first on low, then on high till frothy. Strain into goblets. This drink can be moderated by omitting the lemon juice.

Master Cleanser

This was developed by Stanley Burroughs and is a great way to fast, drinking at least 1 gallon of this a day.

1/4 c	Lemon juice
1/4 c	Maple syrup
1/2 tsp	Cayenne
1 qrt	Water (pure)

The lemon acts as a purifier and toner, the cayenne increases circulation and the maple syrup supplies the necessary glucose to maintain your energy.

ALSO...

In between meals:
Carry with you a 1/2 gallon bottle or thermos full of purified water with the juice of a few lemons. It will cleanse your system, keep you hydrated, and ward off hunger.

⮑ Gorilla Juice ⮐

A high energy, nonfat, after/workout fortifier. The green color is due to the chlorophyll. Isn't it amazing that the Gorilla's awesome strength and gentle nature come from a diet of only raw fruits and vegetables!

Per person:

2 c	**Purified water** (for a sweet version use 1 c water and 1 c pineapple juice)
1 tsp	**Spirulina powder**
	Dash of Cayenne pepper
1 Tbl	**Lemon juice**

Blend well and serve on ice, or chilled.

Sweet Rice Tea

A healthy version of Mexican "horchata." Soaking rice overnight breaks down the starch, making a nourishing chilled drink on hot days, or to accompany hot foods.

1 c	**Organic brown rice, well rinsed**
1 1/2 qrt	**Purified water, with 1/4 c lemon juice squeezed in**
1/4 c	**Honey**
1/2 tsp ea.	**Cardamon, cinnamon, and grated orange peel**
1	**Organic orange, seeded and sliced**

1) Soak rice in 1/2 the water overnight (8-12 hours), in a glass jar or ceramic container.
2) Blend rice with water, strain into a pitcher.
3) Add spices, water and honey to rice, serve on ice, float an orange slice in each glass.

Serves 4

Enlightn' Mint Tea

Fresh squeezed citrus goes well with mint tea, serve chilled or on ice.

6	Mint tea bags (appx. 4 Tbl loose tea)
1 qrt	Water
2	Oranges, juiced (approx. 3/4 c)
1	Lemon, juiced (approx. 1/4 c)
2 Tbl	Honey

Sun tea method: Add tea bags to water in glass jar—let sit in sun for 5 hours or longer, remove tea bags, add rest of ingredients and chill.

Stove method: Steep tea bags in cup of boiling water for 10 minutes. Remove tea bags, stir in honey, pour (or strain) into pitcher, add rest of water and juices—chill.

Makes 6 cups

Hibiscus Cooler

A hot weather tropical drink with a pretty ruby red color.

1/2 c	Hibiscus flowers (dried herb)
1/4 c	Rose hips (dried)
1 1/2 qrt	Water
1 c ea.	Orange juice and pineapple juice
1/4 c	Lemon juice
1/4 c	Honey

1) Cover herbs with 2 c boiling water, cover and let sit 15 minutes, stir in honey and strain into a pitcher.
2) Stir in rest of ingredients, chill and serve on ice.

Garnish with a pineapple wedge or orange slice if desired. Makes 8 1/2 cups.

Easy Nut Milks

Soaking releases and increases the nutrients in nuts making them a more digestible protein, Nut milks also make a healthy alternative cow's milk. Makes 3 1/2 cups.

1/2 c	Almonds or cashews
3 c	Purified water
	(you can add dried fruit to the soak water too: apricots, raisins, dates, etc.)

1) Soak nuts together in water overnight.

2) Blend in blender till creamy (several minutes).

3) Sweeten to taste with honey, barley malt or maple syrup. Strain, serve on ice or serve hot on a cold night; with added cinnamon, cardamon, nutmeg and vanilla.

Carob Almond Milk

Follow directions above using almonds.

Adding

2 Tbl	Honey or maple syrup
1 tsp	Carob powder
1/2 tsp	Vanilla

Strain, chill or serve warm with an extra cup of soymilk added if you desire.

For smoothies

Blend the nut milk with frozen bananas (and protein powder) for a truly delicious shake.

Try these combinations

Almond Apricot with cardamon and nutmeg
Cashew Date with cinnamon
Cashew Banana (Blend a Banana in for extra potassium)

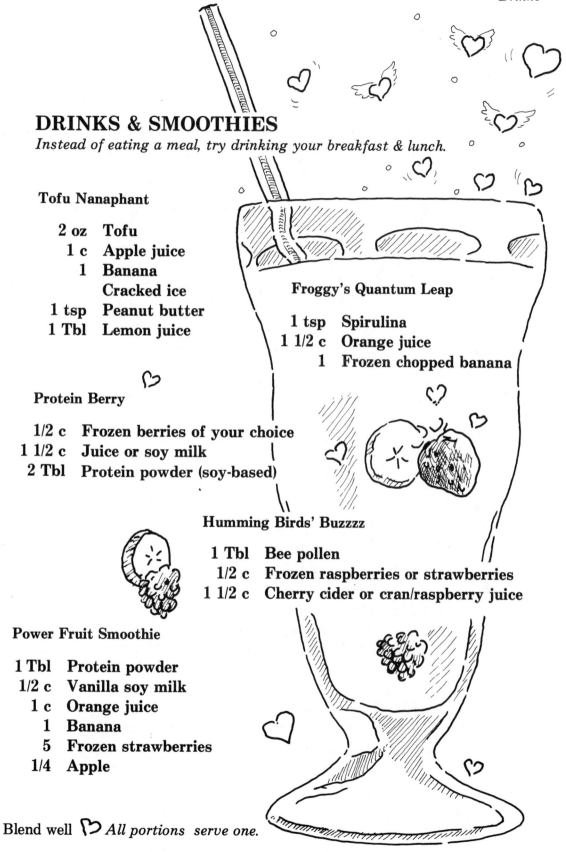

DRINKS & SMOOTHIES

Instead of eating a meal, try drinking your breakfast & lunch.

Tofu Nanaphant

2 oz	Tofu
1 c	Apple juice
1	Banana
	Cracked ice
1 tsp	Peanut butter
1 Tbl	Lemon juice

Froggy's Quantum Leap

1 tsp	Spirulina
1 1/2 c	Orange juice
1	Frozen chopped banana

Protein Berry

1/2 c	Frozen berries of your choice
1 1/2 c	Juice or soy milk
2 Tbl	Protein powder (soy-based)

Humming Birds' Buzzzz

1 Tbl	Bee pollen
1/2 c	Frozen raspberries or strawberries
1 1/2 c	Cherry cider or cran/raspberry juice

Power Fruit Smoothie

1 Tbl	Protein powder
1/2 c	Vanilla soy milk
1 c	Orange juice
1	Banana
5	Frozen strawberries
1/4	Apple

Blend well ♡ *All portions serve one.*

Sunday Scrambler

A yummy brunch star with no cholesterol.

1 Tbl	Aminos
1	Garlic clove, pressed
1/2	Onion, sliced
1 c	Tofu
2 Tbl	Water
	Dash turmeric
1 drop	Toasted sesame oil
1	Tomato

1) Heat aminos in wok or skillet, add garlic, stir quickly.
2) Add onions and spices, saute briefly till tender.
3) Add tofu and water, simmer 5 minutes.
4) Toss in tomato wedges 1 minute before serving.

Serves 2

Tofu Florentine

*Sautéed tofu nestled on a bed of spinach with a **Light Lemon Sauce***
drizzled on top, oil-less, dairy-less and cholesterol free. A light version
of Eggs Florentine.

Per person:

2 oz.	**Tofu (1/2" thick cutlet)**
2 c	**Spinach leaves, packed fresh (or approx. 10 oz. frozen)**
1/4 c	**Light Lemon Sauce***
1 tsp ea.	**Aminos, lemon juice, water**
1 Tbl	**Wine**
	Fresh nutmeg and black pepper

1) Sauté tofu in liquids (not wine) in small skillet, sprinkle on spices. Cook both sides—set aside on another plate.
2) Add spinach leaves and wine to skillet, stir quickly over a medium high heat—only 3-4 minutes.
3) Make a bed of spinach on plate, place tofu filet on top. Drizzle sauce on top. Garnish with a lemon butterfly.**

*See recipe in sauce section
**In culinary decorations

Tofu Rancheros

An egg-less, oil-less version of Huevos (eggs) Rancheros. This country style dish layers a tortilla, tofu, and chile sauce and tops it with soy cheese, onions, peppers or whatever you wish. Serve with rice and beans, or fresh fruit for a hearty brunch. Make the sauce ahead for a quick morning preparation.

Per person:

1	**Corn tortilla**
1 tsp	**Aminos**
1 tsp	**Water**
2 oz	**Firm tofu (1/2" thick cutlet)**
1/4 c	**Sliced red onions**
1/4 c	**Chile Roja Enchilada Sauce*, warmed**
1/4 c	**Soy cheese, grated**
	Garnish of choice: peppers, green onions, avocados, black olives, sprouts, etc.

1) Toast tortilla until crisp.
2) Sauté tofu in Aminos and water, cook both sides, add onions, stir for 2 minutes more. Set aside onto a dish.
3) Put crisp tortilla in skillet, arrange tofu on top, pour sauce on top, and add soy cheese, cover and turn to low until soy cheese melts (just a couple of minutes).
4) Slide onto a plate and garnish.

*You can also serve this with **Meximato sauce**.

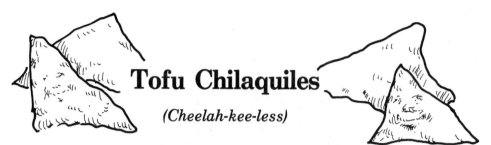

Tofu Chilaquiles

(Cheelah-kee-less)

An intoxicating way to use up leftover tortillas. Delicious for Sunday Brunch or lighter meals. Serves 2-3.

1/2 dz	**Corn tortillas**
1/2 lb	**Firm tofu**
1/2 c	**Salsa Verde or Chile Verde Sauce—see recipe**
1/2 c	**Soy jack cheese**
1/2 Tbl	**Water**
1/2	**Onion**
1 Tbl	**Aminos**

1) Halve tortillas, then cut into 1/2" strips. Cut tofu into 1/2" cubes and slice onion. Toast tortilla strips in oven till slightly crisp.
2) Heat wok, add aminos and water, add tortillas strips and sauté on high stirring fast till crisp and meaty.
3) Add sliced onion, tofu and aminos, continue stirring.
4) Add soy cheese and 1/4 c of sauce, stir then cover on low, heat for a few minutes.
5) Serve with heated sauce on top and a cilantro garnish.

Serve with **Yucatan Fruit Salad** *and sparkling juice beverage.*

Breakfast Apple Torte

This looks and tastes sensational.
For dessert, try topping it with vanilla soy ice cream.

4	Apples, medium size
2 Tbl	Soya lecithin spread
1 Tbl	Egg replacer mixed with 4 Tbl water
3/4 c	Vanilla soy milk
1/2 c	Whole wheat pastry flour
1 tsp	Vanilla

Cinnamon and honey drizzled on top

1) Peel, core and thinly slice apples—preheat oven 375°.
2) Beat egg replacer with water, add soymilk and vanilla, stir in flour.
3) Heat soya lecithin in baking dish or skillet till melted. Arrange apples in a swirl pattern and pour batter on top.
4) Swirl on honey and cinnamon bake 350° for 15 min.

Serves 4-5

Morning Fruit Crisp

A quick breakfast treat using fresh fruit.

Per person:

      1 c   **Peaches, apricots, pears, any fresh fruit in season**
    1/4 c   **Granola of choice**
    1 Tbl   **Natural fruit syrup**
              Soy milk

1) Slice fruit of choice, arrange on a baking dish.
2) Sprinkle granola on top, swirling a little syrup over it.
3) Bake at 350° for 20 min.
4) Serve in bowls with soymilk if desired.

Müesli

Prepare the night before or let sit an hour or two before serving.

Per person serving:

    1 tsp   **Honey or apple concentrate**
     1/2   **Apple, grated**
    1/4c   **Whole grain flakes (oat, rye, wheat or mixture)**
    1 Tbl   **Ground flax seed**
    1 Tbl   **Oatbran**
              Soaked raisins and almonds

Mix all together and let soak in either soy yogurt, apple juice or soymilk. Spice it as you like with cinnamon, vanilla or maple extract. Serve with fresh fruit on top.

The Universal Tofu Pancake

No eggs or oil in this nourishing thin pancake.

1 pack	Silken tofu (10.5 oz.)
1/2 c	Vanilla soy milk
1 Tbl	Honey
1/2	Banana
1/2 c	Wholewheat pastry flour

1) Blend everything till smooth.
2) Heat non-stick griddle on medium heat (a light oil coating might be necessary).
3) Pour on batter and heat till golden, flip and heat other side. The first couple of cakes sometimes won't turn out, but don't despair because they get the griddle in gear for the best ones.
4) Serve with maple syrup, fruit syrup or fresh fruit and soy yogurt.

Serves approximately 4

Vanilla Fruit Crepes

1	Recipe tofu pancakes prepared as above
	Soy vanilla yogurt, stirred well
	Fresh fruit or berries of choice (sliced peaches, apricots or strawberries are superb)

1) Spread batter on hot griddle as thin as possible making large circles.
2) Assemble: Put soy yogurt and fruit inside or soy yogurt inside and roll up with fruit on top, whichever way sounds good to you.
3) Warm in oven before serving or serve'em as you make'em.

Blue Corn Raspberry Muffins

Blue corn contains more nutrients than yellow corn.

1 c	**Blue corn meal**
1 c	**Whole wheat pastry flour**
1 Tbl	**Soy protein powder (increases protein)**
3 tsp	**Cinnamon**
1/4 tsp	**Fresh grated nutmeg**
1 c	**Apple juice**
1 Tbl	**Egg replacer mixed with 4 Tbl water**
1/4 c	**Walnuts chopped**
1/2 c	**Fresh or frozen raspberries**

1) Mix first 4 ingredients, add rest of items and spoon into lightly oiled muffin tin.
2) Bake 375° for 20 minutes, makes 1 dozen.

Zucchini Raisin Muffins

Delicate zucchinis make these muffins moist.

1/4 c	Raisins
1/2 c ea.	Bran and boiling water
1/2 c	Orange juice
1/3 c	Honey
2 c	Shredded zucchinis
1 Tbl	Egg replacer mixed with 4 Tbl water
1 c	Whole wheat pastry flour
1/2 c	Blue or yellow corn meal
4 tsp	Baking powder
2 tsp	Cinnamon

1) Let raisins and bran soak in water, preheat oven to 375.°
2) Stir orange juice, honey, zucchinis and egg replacer, stir into raisin bran mix.
3) Stir separately the dry ingredients then fold into wet mix.
4) Pour into oiled muffin tin and bake 375° for 20 minutes.

Makes 12 muffins.

Layered Maple Oat Muffins

A delicious way to eat oat bran.

1 c	Oat bran
3/4 c	Soy milk
1 1/2 tsp	Egg replacer mixed with 2 Tbl water
1/4 c	Soya lecithin spread
2	Ripe bananas
1 c	Unbleached or whole wheat pastry flour
2 1/2 tsp	Baking soda
1 tsp	Baking powder
1/2 c	Maple syrup
1/2 c	Walnuts or almonds, ground
2 Tbl	Whole wheat pastry flour
1 tsp	Cinnamon

1) Put oatbran in soy milk till absorbed, preheat oven at 400°.
2) Beat in egg replacer.
3) Add soya spread and bananas, beat well.
4) In a separate bowl mix flour with soda and baking powder, then add to above mixture until just barely mixed. Mix in separate bowl the last 4 items.
5) Lightly oil a muffin tin and fill 1/4 full with batter, then alternate with maple filling until muffin is full.
6) Bake 400° for 20 minutes.

Makes 1 dozen

Apple Oatbran Muffins

A moist and delicious muffin without eggs or oil, producing a very light texture.

3 c   Oatbran (rice or wheat bran can substitute)
1 c   Boiling water
3 tsp   Egg replacer mixed with 4 Tbl water
3/4 c   Rice syrup, barley malt syrup or honey
2 c   Soymilk
1 c   Toasted black walnuts
2 c   Whole wheat pastry flour
1/2 tsp   Cinnamon and clove powder
2 1/2 tsp   Soda
2 c   Grated apple

1) Let the bran soak in water till absorbed, preheat oven 375°.
2) Beat egg replacer, honey, soy milk and mix into bran mixture, add apples.
3) Sift together dry ingredients and fold into other batter.
4) Pour into greased muffin tin and bake 375° for 25 minutes—makes 1 dozen. Covered batter keeps in refrigerator for several weeks.

Pineapple Nut Oatbran Muffins

Follow recipe above and add instead of apple,

2 c   Chunk pineapple (instead of 2 c apple)
1/2 c   Date sugar instead of honey
   Delete clove powder

Also, macadamia nuts are a nice substitute for walnuts.

Müesli Muffins

Yields 1 dozen healthy, easy to prepare muffins.

Preheat oven at 400°

1 lb	Tofu, soft
1/2 c	Orange juice, fresh
2 Tbl	Honey
1/4 c	Fructose
1	Banana
1 tsp	Vanilla
1 Tbl	Baking powder
1 tsp	Baking soda
1 c	Whole wheat pastry flour
1 1/4 c	Müesli (whole grain flakes with raisins)

1) Blend first six items in a blender or food processor.
2) In another bowl sift dry items together.
3) Gently fold dry into wet, spoon into greased muffin tins and bake at 375° for 20 minutes or until toothpick inserted comes out clean.

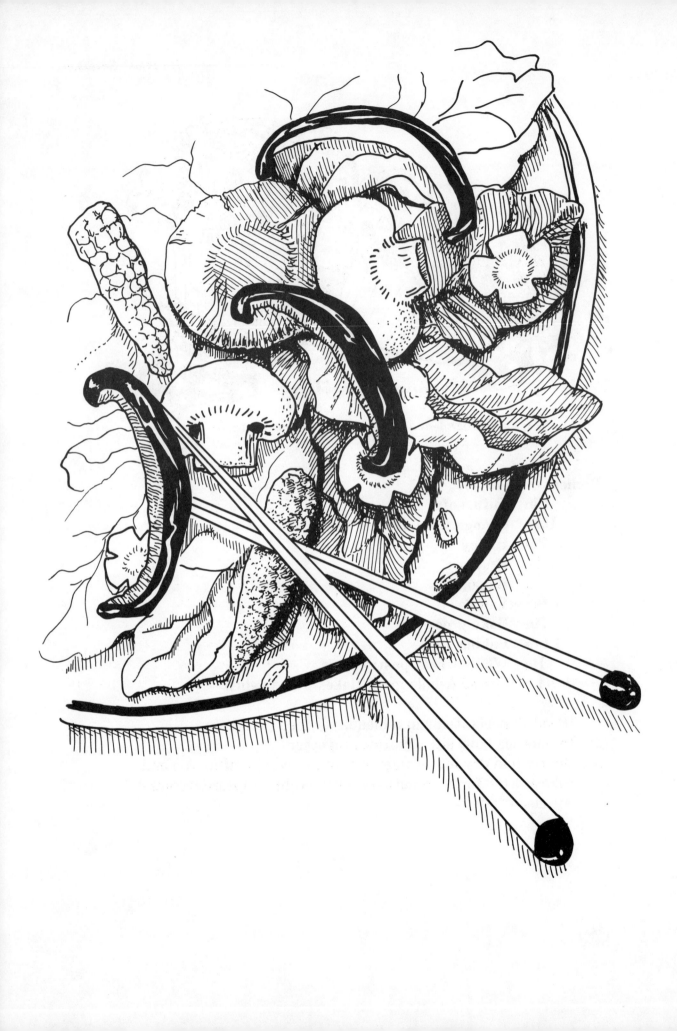

SALADS

SALADS

Fruits and vegetables are some of the most abundant, nourishing and giving friends we have. They come to us in so many luscious and colorful varieties. They are best eaten right out of the garden or off the trees, so search out the farmers markets and organic grocers near you to enjoy the freshest, tastiest produce possible. Raw vegetables and fruits are so good for you. They are an abundant source of fiber, vitamins, minerals and enzymes. Try eating more fresh fruits and vegetables, substituting a crunchy raw carrot for chips and see the difference it makes: you'll feel lighter and brighter.

May these recipes spark your culinary creativity and send you on many tasty travels through the Garden of Eatin'.

Color, Texture & Flavor

The human spirit cannot be contained. As the walls dissolve that have separated the nations, we experience the synthesis of One Great Humanity. As we welcome our mighty multi-cultural world, we also welcome the dynamic variety of foods from around the globe. This endless exploration of new flavors, textures and colors enlivens and expands our senses, through preparing the traditional and in combining for the new. Be adventurous! Experiment with foods you've never tried, letting your imagination play in the great abundance of variety.

May the following ideas ignite your own culinary exploration of transforming ordinary foods into a work of art.

Here are some thoughts regarding the color, texture and flavor of food, as living sculptures of the Divine.

Color

The color of whole natural food, like all living things, is the expression of white light through the spectrum, each color transmitting an energy vibration. Color is a feast for the eyes; healing mind, body, and soul, as well as appetizing to the palate. Balance the colors in a meal, use red, orange, yellow, green, blue, purple and white for a visual delight. Eating foods according to their color is an aspect of the Rainbow Diet: relying upon the outer color or vibration of food to correspond to the chakras (energy centers) of the body[5].

For example, red foods, (red apples, strawberries, etc.) link to the base or lower chakra and energize the system. Green foods (green leafy plants and vegetables) promote calmness and are healing to the heart chakra. Blue foods (blueberries, blue corn, potatoes, grapes) link to the throat chakra and enhance our creativity[6]. Also try eating warm colored foods (red, orange and yellow) in the morning and cool colors later on in the day (green, blue and purple). Use white-gold foods (soy products, grains, papaya, etc.) with any meal.

Use complementary colors to enhance and excite your visual display of meals. From red, yellow and blue, one can derive all colors. These are the primary colors. Mix primaries to create secondary colors: yellow and red create orange, red and blue create purple, blue and yellow create green. Have fun visually complementing foods with this easy way of determining color opposites:

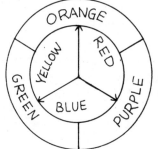

To discover the opposite complementary color of red tomatoes for example, mix the remaining two primaries (yellow and blue) to find green. Use green leaves, herbs or vegetables to visually complement red tomatoes. Yellow vegetables should be accented with something purple, like grated beets or red cabbage. Enliven an orange salad with blueberries.

Blue/orange, red/green, and purple/yellow themes produce electric and beautiful contrasts. Painters play off these opposites to create more vividness in their paintings, opposites vibrate each other and become more brilliant than if placed next to similar colors.

Colors truly are nourishing light rays, dynamically enhancing our daily life.

Texture

Texture is the surface arrangement of your food and is fun to vary. In one dish meals such as mandala salads, cut your vegetables in different ways. You can create a masterpiece by shredding one vegetable, cutting, tearing or mincing others. For special occasions try cutting a star or flower shape out of carrots, carve moons out of cucumbers, sliver zucchinis so long and fine that they resemble pasta. Combine the natural beauty of whole foods with the art of cutting. This is a zen approach to food presentation as in Ikeban, the Japanese Art of flower arranging. Work with nature to create inspiring edible art for the soul. (See "Culinary Decorations", page 61, for a guide to garnishes and cutting ideas.)

Flavors

A rich melody of tastes are created by combining different flavors. More attentive smelling will exhalt and educate your taste buds, since taste and smell work in tandem. Balancing sweet, salty, sour and spicy is an art to learn through practice and tasting. Discover these alternatives: for **hot**; try cayenne pepper, horseradish, and all chiles fresh or dried. For **sweet**; there is honey, maple syrup, concentrated fruit juices, fresh and dried fruit, barley malt and rice syrup. **Salty** alternatives are liquid aminos, miso, umeboshi paste, tamari, sea salt, and Bronner's liquid soy bouillon. **Sour** is found in citrus (limes and lemons) and vinegars.

Pungent and **spicy** flavors are garlic, ginger, onion, curry powders, cumin, chiles and other dried spices.

To bring out the flavor of root vegetables (carrots, beets, turnips, radishes) and make them easier to digest when eaten raw, increase the surface area by finely grating them in the food processor.

Natural flavors are truly the best. Use herbs and spices to accent foods rather than fats and oils. Herbs are less fattening, cleaner and easier for your system to digest. Also experiment with the different flavors that wines bring to food. The quality of the wines essence will linger long after the evaporation of the alcohol.

By creating and experiencing new flavors and tastes in our food preparation, we awaken the full potential of our senses through the foods that we eat.

Cutting Techniques

A basic visual guide to common cuts.

Angled cuts

Hold knife at an angle pointed away from you, as you slice the vegetables.

Chop

Cut in uniform pieces, approx. 1/2″ thick.

Course chop

Larger cuts, from approx. 1″ thick.

Crush

Use a blender or coffee/nut grinder to pulverize whole seeds, pods, herbs and spices. Crushing spices prior to usage produces the freshest flavors and releases wonderful aromas in your kitchen.

Cube or dice

Small cube-shaped sections are made by slicing horizontally in 1/2″ intervals, then slicing vertical at 1/2″ intervals. Dicing is a smaller version of the cube.

Julienne

Cutting vegetables horizontally at 1/4″ intervals, then cut lengthwise into match sticks. Named after the French chef Julien in 1785.

Mince

Finely dice using a large knife or cleaver, continue scraping food into a mound and chop until all pieces are a uniform 1/16″-1/8″ size.

Slice

Cut into 1/4″ wide sections.

Sliver

Cut into 1/16″-1/8″ wide sections.

Shred

Use a grater or food processor (grate blade) to shear thin sections off carrots, cabbage or beets, making them easier to eat raw in salad form.

Culinary Decorations

A garnish can be as simple as a parsley sprig, or as complex as carving a swan out of a block of ice. There are many ways to transform your meal into a work of art with little effort.

Here are a few fun ways to create new shapes out of ordinary foods. Wash your produce before beginning and use sharp utencils.

Radish UFO's
Slice radish into disks, cut a slice halfway through, fit two sliced edges together, like two intersecting planes.

Zucchini Flowers
Slice zucchini lengthwise into 1/8″ thickness, then cut small slices along one edge—creating a "comb" effect. Twirl it around, spiraling it from the outside in, to make a flower shape. Lay a red grape in the center.

Lemon lime butterflies
Slice thinly and cut triangles or 1/2 moons out of citrus. Place 2 edges together and use a thin chive or red pepper strip as antennae.

Chile Flowers
Slice lengthwise into strips leaving stems attached, shake out seeds. Put in ice water until tips curl out.

Rose buds
Trim bottom off radishes so they can sit flat. Slice 4-5 petals around radish perimeter. Pare center into an oval. Chill in ice water until petals open. Make large roses from turnips by cutting petals all around perimeter.

Carrot ribbons

Peel carrot and use a paring knife to peel off thick peels or "ribbons." Roll each peel up into a curl and place into a small ice cube tray. Put in freezer for an hour, then unwind and twist ribbons onto plates.

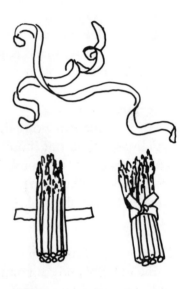

Leek laces

Cook leek leaves until tender. Cut into 6-7" lengths and place on plates. Place steamed asparagus, carrot or yellow squash strips on top and tie leek laces around them creating a bundle.

Pepper triangles

Use red, yellow or green pepper sections (2″x3″ flat shape) to create fun triangles. Make 1 cut halfway up pepper on opposing sides, twist and pull apart into a triangle shape.

Carrot sticks and flowers

Cut 4 "V" shapes lengthwise down carrot— a 4-petaled "flower" will be left after you make thin slices across carrot.

Yucatan Fruit Salad

A superb complement to Mexican main dishes (i.e, enchiladas, rellenos)
this is the first course to be devoured.

         2 c   **Fresh pineapple**
       1 sm   **Jicama**
        1 lg   **Mango (not too soft)**
      1 tsp   **Jalapeño pepper, chopped**
      2 Tbl   **Packed cilantro leaves**
            1   **Lime, juiced**
      1 tsp   **Poppy seeds**

1)   Chop pineapple, jicama and mango, put in bowl.
2)   Put jalapeño chunks through a garlic press and press juice onto
       fruit, discard the fibers inside the press.
3)   Chop cilantro leaves and add with rest of spices.

Chill.

Hawaiian Pineapple Boats

The pineapple shell becomes the serving bowl in this pretty party salad.

  1 lg   **Pineapple**
    3   **Bananas**
    3   **Kiwis**
  18   **Strawberries**

1) Slice pineapple lengthwise, cut core out of each half. Cut out pineapple into chunks. Set aside in medium bowl.
2) Slice rest of fruit, add to bowl with pineapple.
3) Fill pineapple halves and decorate with long spears from pineapple cores, or you can cut cores into shapes and hold with tooth picks.

Papaya Kiwi Salad

A refreshing and delightful salad that also makes a great light dessert,
excellent for digestion.

1	**Papaya (or half a Mexican papaya)**
1-2	**Kiwis**
1/4 c	**Raisins**
1	**Lime, cut in half (juice one half, quarter other half)**

1) Peel and slice papaya into small spears, peel and quarter kiwis.
2) Arrange on a beautiful platter and sprinkle with raisins and lime juice.

Serve 1/2 the lime in wedges on the side.

Serves 2-4.

Independence Day Salad

A Red, White & Blue Salad

1 basket	**Strawberries**
2	**Bananas**
1/2 basket	**Blueberries**

1) Slice bananas and strawberries
2) Toss all in a bowl for a red white and blue salute.

Top with applesauce or a honey-lemon juice sauce if desired.

Serves 2-4.

Peter Rabbit's Salad

Kids will hop for this one!

1 lg	Carrot
1 1/2	Yellow apples
1/2 c	Raisins
1/3 c	Vanilla "soygurt"*
1 Tbl	Lemon juice
dash	Cinnamon
1/3 c	Chopped toasted walnuts (optional)

1) Grate the carrot and apple in food processor.
2) Pour boiling water over raisins to make them plump—strain after 5 minutes.
3) Toss it all together.

* Note: You can make your own vanilla soygurt by adding a bit of vanilla extract and honey or maple syrup to plain soy yogurt.

MANDALA SALADS

The visual arrangement of salads can be designed to symbolize the wheels of the universe. Constructing symmetrical artful salads can be a fun way to be creative and exceptionally delightful to delve into.

Traditionally, mandalas have been created by native folk peoples as an aid to meditation and as a vehicle for teaching their spiritual oneness with all. Creating mandalas is a ceremony in itself. See it as a sacred presentation for yourself and loved ones, each molecule of food being a crystal of love.

For a vegetable mandala, begin with a large platter or dish, and place spinach, lettuce or beet greens around the perimeter. Continue whirling this spiral flower with the vegetables that please you, such as finely shredded roots, julienne zucchinis, cucumber spears and sprouts. End in the center with something beautiful, like a radish "flower" (*see diagram in *Culinary Decorations*). For a fruit mandala, place lettuce leaves around perimeter, spiral fresh fruits in a pleasing pattern, and decorate with soaked dried fruit and nuts.

As you create a beautiful salad, remember that we too create our lives, what a gift!

Red Cabbage Slaw

This makes a large bowl of nourishing slaw, the Balsamic vinaigrette complements the red cabbage.

1	Lg. carrot
1/2	Red cabbage
1/8	Green cabbage
1	Cucumber
	Few fresh sprigs of basil leaves

Balsamic Vinaigrette

2 Tbl	Lemon juice
1	Heaping spoonful of a light, eggless, or tofu mayo
1	Garlic clove, pressed
	Balsamic vinegar to thin

1) Shred carrot and cabbages. Skin, seed and chop the cucumber, tear basil leaves in small pieces.
2) Whisk or stir sauce with a fork, and toss all together.

Grated Beet Salad

Figure 1 beet per person. This salad is simple and refreshing!

4-5	Grated beets (approx. 2 c)
2-3 Tbl	Dilled rice vinegar
	Add radish sprouts and fresh green peas for a a more complex and varied salad

1) Grate beets finely (a fine-shred food processor blade works the best), toss with vinegar.

If you can't find the vinegar make your own by adding fresh or dried dill weed to natural rice vinegar, be sure to read the label since "seasoned" rice vinegar contains sugar.

Fennel Cabbage Slaw

The fragrance of fresh herbs with the sweetness of fennel provides a wonderful combination.

2 sm	Zucchinis
1	Yellow crook neck squash
2	Carrots
1	Fennel bulb
1/2	Head cabbage
1 Tbl	Fresh dill, minced
1 Tbl	Toasted sun seeds (optional)

1) Slice zucchini in rounds, julienne the squash, thinly slice carrots, shred fennel and cabbage.
2) Toss in a bowl with **Creamy Dill Dressing** *(see recipe p. 109),* add dill and seeds.

Indian Carrot Salad

This low calorie salad uses garam masala and soygurt for a unique taste.

3 lg	Carrots
1/3 c	Raisins, soaked in
2 Tbl	Apple juice
1	Banana, not too soft
1/2	Lemon, juiced
2 Tbl	Soygurt
1 tsp	Garam masala*, p. 156

1) Shred carrots finely in food processor.
2) Slice bananas.
3) Stir everything together. *Chill.*

*Garam Masala *is an Indian seasoning blend of many flavors; it imparts a roasted, nutty, spicy taste.*

Ginger Lentil Sprout Salad

Crunchy, refreshing and vitamin packed, this Japanese flavored salad nestles mineral rich nori and hiziki seaweed with lentil sprouts for a great light meal.

2 1/2 c	Sprouted lentils
1/2 c	Celery, finely chopped
1/2	Red onion, minced (approx. 1/3 c)
1 Tbl	Ginger, fresh, minced
1 1/2 Tbl	Soy sauce (or tamari)
1/2 Tbl	Toasted Sesame oil—optional
1 1/2 Tbl	Lemon juice
3 sheets	Nori, toasted and torn into small pieces
1/4 c	Soaked hiziki

Toss and chill, garnish with minced green onions.

Serves 2-3

Chinese Snap Pea Salad

1/2 lb	Snap peas, whole
1 c	Sliced red peppers
2 Tbl	Red onion, minced
1 Tbl	Brown sesame seeds

Sauce

	Juice of 1 orange
1 Tbl	Mellow white miso
1	Garlic clove, crushed
1 tsp	Honey or pure maple syrup or rice syrup
1 tsp	Rice vinegar

1) Steam peas whole 5 minutes—should be crisp tender.
2) Put peas with rest of ingredients in a medium bowl.
3) Stir sauce together then pour over vegetables.

Chill.

Sunflower Sprout Salad

2 c	Sprouted sunflower seeds
3/4 c	Red cabbage, shredded
3/4 c	Green cabbage, diced
1/4 c	Cilantro leaves
1/4 c	Balsamic vinegar or vinaigrette
	Cherry tomato halves as garnish

Toss everything together, chill.

Mediterranean Eggplant Salad

*This hearty salad goes well with crusty bread,
and a tossed green leaf salad.*

1 lg	Whole eggplant, skinned and diced (approx. 1 1/2 lb.)
1 med	Onion, diced
2	Garlic cloves, minced
1/4 c	Lemon juice
1 ea.	Red pepper, green pepper, julienne
1/4 c	Parsley, chopped
1	Can garbanzos (approx. 15 oz.)
2 Tbl	Olive oil
1 Tbl	Oregano
	Pinch of cayenne and sea salt

1) Steam first two ingredients till tender.
2) Toss rest of ingredients in a medium bowl, add eggplant mix and chill.

Marinated Vegetables

Makes a great snack.

1/2	Head cauliflower, cut into florettes
1 c	Carrots, sliced thinly
1	Red onion, sliced thinly
1 c	Cherry tomatoes, halved
1	Stalk broccoli, cut into floretts, peel and chop stems
4	Zucchinis, sliced (approx. 1 lb.)

1) Parboil carrots and broccoli, no more than 2 minutes.
2) Toss the vegetables with 1 1/2 cups of the low-cal garlic herb dressing and chill several hours or overnight.

Cauliflower Almond Salad

A yummy salad with toasted almonds.

1	Big cauliflower
1/2 lg	Onion
1	Bell pepper, sliced
1/2 c	Almonds
2	Garlic cloves, pressed
1/2	Lemon, juiced
1 Tbl	Liquid aminos (or 1/2 Tbl Tamari with 1/2 Tbl water)
1/4 c	Tofu-mayo sauce

1) Tear cauliflower into florettes, slice onion and steam together for 3-5 min., rinse in cold water.
2) Put in bowl with bell peppers.
3) Chop and toast almonds.
4) Toss all ingredients and enjoy!

Coyote's Beet-loaf Salad

A nutritious blend of grated vegetables, nuts, tofu and spices formed into a festive southwestern shape. A complete meal in itself.

2	**Beets**
2	**Carrots**
1/4	**Head cabbage**
1	**Zucchini (approx. 6″length)**
4	**Green onions**
1	**Bell pepper**
1	**Garlic clove**
2 Tbl	**Cilantro leaves**
1/8 c	**Aminos**
1/2 c	**Sunflower seeds**
1/4 c	**Almonds**
1/2 c	**Tofu**
2 Tbl	**Flax seeds**
1/4 c	**Nutritional yeast**
1 tsp	**Cumin**
1/2 tsp ea.	**Chile powder and seasalt**

1) Shred all vegetables in food processor or by hand.
2) Toast seeds lightly in oven, finely grind in blender—stop and stir occasionally till all is ground.
3) Mix everything in bowl, then form into a cactus or moon, garnish with sliced olives, avocadoes, tomatoes and cilantro, serve with chips & salsa and **Salsa Creme** dressing, p. 105.

Delphi Spinach Salad

- 1 Bunch spinach
- 1/2 Cucumber, skinned
- Several cherry tomatoes, halved
- 6 Black olives, sliced
- 2 oz. Soy cheese, crumbled
- 3 Tbl Sunflower seeds, freshly toasted
- Lemon wedges

1) Rinse, drain and pat spinach leaves dry, tear into a large bowl or platter.
2) Add sliced cucumbers, tomatoes and rest of ingredients.

Serve with vinaigrette dressing.

Black-Eyed Pea Salad

- 4 c Water
- 1 c Black-eyed Peas
- 4 Cloves of garlic, pressed
- 1 Bell pepper
- 1 Jalapeño minced
- 1 sm Onion, thinly sliced
- 1 Red pepper
- 1/2 tsp Sea salt
- 1 tsp Liquid aminos

1) Bring water to boil, add black-eyed peas.
2) Cover, return to a boil, then reduce heat and let sit 2 hours.
3) Bring to boil and simmer 40 minutes.
4) Add chopped peppers and rest of ingredients and toss.

Chill.

Sprouted Soy Salad

A very nourishing salad.

3 c   Soybean sprouts
3   Carrots
1/2 Bell pepper

*Dressing—See "Secrets of the East"

1) Steam sprouts for 3 minutes (available at oriental markets— or grow your own with long tails).
2) Finely grate carrots—food processors are best, chop pepper.
3) Toss in bowl with **Secrets of the East*** dressing.

Three-Herb Tabouli

Quick and easy, a House favorite.

1 c   Cracked wheat (Bulgar)
3/4 c Boiling water
1 Tbl Olive oil
3 Tbl Lemon juice
4 lg   Roma tomatoes, chopped
1 c   Parsley, fresh, loose pack, chopped
2   Scallions, minced
1/2 c Fresh mint, minced
1   Garlic clove, pressed
1 tsp Oregano
       Cracked black pepper and seasalt to taste

1) Pour water over wheat in medium bowl, stir and cover for 20 min.
2) Add rest of ingredients, toss well and chill.

Serve on a bed of baby greens or spinach leaves with sliced lemon wedges and cucumber spears.

Sprouted Lentil Loaf

Salad:

1	Celery stock (use inner soft ribs and leaves only)
1/2	Red onion (1/3-1/2 c)
1 1/2 c	Lentil sprouts
2	Carrots (medium size, approx. 1 c grated)
1/2	Zucchini (approx. 1/3 c)

Sauce:

1/3 c	Tofu mayo
3 Tbl	Lemon juice
2 tsp	Soy sauce or aminos
1	Garlic clove
2 tsp	Dill weed and coriander (if fresh use 1 Tbl each)
	Dash of cumin, curry and cayenne

1) Pulse chop celery and onion finely in food processor. Add lentil sprouts and pulse chop one to three quick times (do not mash).
2) Change blade to a fine grate, grate carrots and zucchinis into same work bowl. Transfer to salad bowl.
3) Blend all sauce ingredients together, toss into salad—form into a loaf and garnish or keep as a tossed salad, chill.

Serves 4

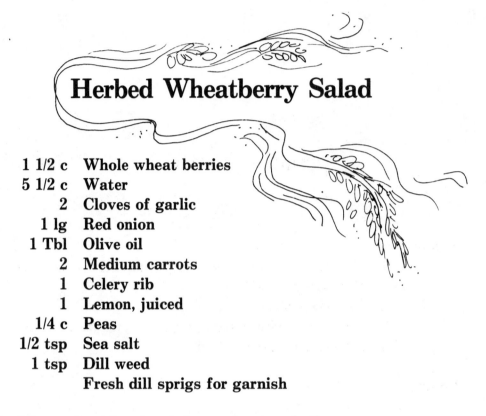

Herbed Wheatberry Salad

1 1/2 c	Whole wheat berries
5 1/2 c	Water
2	Cloves of garlic
1 lg	Red onion
1 Tbl	Olive oil
2	Medium carrots
1	Celery rib
1	Lemon, juiced
1/4 c	Peas
1/2 tsp	Sea salt
1 tsp	Dill weed
	Fresh dill sprigs for garnish

1) Rinse wheat berries, bring water to a boil.
2) Add wheatberries, return to boil and simmer approximately 1 hour.
3) Press garlic, chop onion, and sauté in oil and lemon juice until soft (2 min.). Add to cooked wheat berries.
4) Grate carrots, slice celery.
5) Toss all in bowl and chill.

Serve with a garnish of marinated tomatoes and mushrooms

Pacific Rim Millet Salad

A spicey fragrant tofu and millet salad, delicious as a main course or lunch. Millet is high in protein and is a non-mucus forming grain.

2 c	Cooked millet
1 c	Cubed firm tofu, marinated
1	Red pepper, julienne
1	Lime, juiced
1	Lemon, juiced
1	Jalapeño, roasted and minced
1 sm.	Garlic clove
1 tsp	Fresh minced ginger
2	Green onions, slivered on angle
2 Tbl	Sesame oil
1 Tbl	Toasted sesame seeds
2 tsp	Aminos

Toss and chill (leave seeds in jalapeño if you like spicy foods.)

Spanish Rice Salad

Fragrant rice sautéed in salsa with zucchinis.

3/4 c	Long grain rice (jasmine is my favorite, it has a delicious aroma)
1/2	Lemon
1 1/2 c	Water or broth
1 tsp	Olive oil
1 tsp	Cumin seeds
2	Heaping spoonfuls of salsa fresca (fresh chunkie kind)
1	Garlic, pressed
2-3	Zucchinis, sliced
1 tsp	Coriander
	Tamari to taste

1) Put rice in colander, pour boiling water over it, rinse and drain and repeat.
2) Squeeze lemon on top and cover for 10 minutes or until rice softens.
3) Heat oil in skillet, add rice, continue stirring until it begins to absorb oil and slightly brown.
4) Add salsa, cumin and garlic; continue stirring then add water or broth, zucchinis and tamari , cover for 15 minutes.
5) Fluff with a fork when done.
6) Put into a bowl and toss with:

2-3	Sprigs fresh chopped Basil leaves
1 Tbl	Toasted sesame seeds
1	Tomato, seeded and chopped
	Sliced green olives to taste

Three-Pepper Black Bean

A festive and fragrant salad, dotted with yellow, red and green peppers.

2 c	Cooked black beans
1	Clove, garlic
1/2″	Square piece ginger
2/3 c	Yellow pepper
2/3 c	Green pepper
2/3 c	Red pepper
1/4 c	Cilantro leaves
1/3 c	Green onions (approx. 3)
1 tsp	Each vinegar and aminos
	Cracked pepper to taste (if you like spicy—add cayenne or a jalapeño pressed)
	Cucumber
	Tomato
	Onion/Alfalfa sprouts

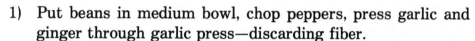

1) Put beans in medium bowl, chop peppers, press garlic and ginger through garlic press—discarding fiber.
2) Chop cilantro and mince onions—add to bowl, stir well and chill.

Before serving:
3) Seed, skin and chop cucumbers in half moons, wedge tomatoes.
4) On a serving platter, lay a ring of sprouts, put bean salad in center then arrange tomatoes and cucumbers around perimeter.

Marinated Bean Salad

To turn into a sensational salad, spoon over a bed of shredded greens, chopped tomatoes and peppers, with your choice of dressing.

1 1/2 c	Baby lima beans (you can use any beans)
1 Tbl	Minced ginger
2	Cloves, garlic
	Bay leaf

1) Cover beans with water and soak overnight.
2) Rinse beans, cover with fresh water and bring to a boil, then reduce to simmer 45 min. to 1 hour until al dente (not mushy soft).
3) Drain in colander and rinse in cold water.
4) Put in a large bowl and toss with:

2	Garlic cloves, pressed
2 Tbl	Olive oil
1 Tbl	Italian herbs (a mix of oregano, basil, rosemary and thyme)
1/2	Lemon juiced, with thinly sliced sections for garnish
1/4 tsp	Sea salt
1 Tbl	Liquid aminos
2 Tbl	Red wine vinegar

Santa Fe Tempeh Salad

For a festive summer meal try this salad with toasted corn tortillas, refried beans or bean dip, fresh fruit or **Yucatan Salad.**

8 oz	Tempeh, steamed
1/2 c	Almonds, roasted then chopped
1 lg	Tomato, chopped
1	Bell pepper, thinly sliced
1/2 bunch	Cilantro, chopped (approx. 1/4 c)
2	Limes, juiced
1/2	Red onion, minced
2	Tangerines, sectioned and peeled
1 lg	Garlic clove, pressed
2 Tbl	Tamari or aminos
1/4 tsp	Cayenne (or 1/2 jalapeño, minced)
1/2 tsp	Chili powder

1) Cube steamed tempeh, pour tamari, chili, garlic and cayenne over it and toss—let sit an hour or two or overnight to absorb flavor.

2) Chop all veggies and toss together in large container—chill.

Salad for a Mermaid

1 c	Hiziki seaweed
1 1/2 c	Peas
3	Small carrots
1/2 c	Tofu, cut in 1/2″ cubes
	A few cilantro leaves, chopped

Sauce

2 Tbl	Tamari
1/4 c	Fresh ginger
1 1/2 tsp	Toasted sesame oil
1 tsp	Wasabi powder
1	Green onion
1/2 c	Water
1/4 c	Lemon juice
1 Tbl	Sesame tahini
2 tsp	Honey

1) Soak hiziki in hot water for 10 minutes, rinse and drain.
2) Steam peas a few minutes till tender.
3) Cut carrots into "sticks and flowers." *See diagram in* **Culinary Decorations**.
4) Toss vegetables, then blend sauce in blender till smooth and strain over salad—discard fiber in strainer.

Chill

Citrus Pasta Salad

A refreshing yet fiery salad full of unusual tastes.

4 oz	Fresh spaghetti or soba noodles
2	Oranges, peeled and chopped
1/2 c	Nopalitos*, diced
1 c	Pineapple chunks, fresh
1	Lime, juiced
1/2-1	Jalapeño, minced

1) Cook pasta al dente.
2) Toss with the rest in a bowl and be prepared for a very interesting experience.

Nopalitos are cactus pads, usually found skinned, diced and canned in the Mexican section of markets.

Veggie Rotelli in Parsley Sauce

10 oz.	Rotelli pasta
8 oz.	Mushrooms, sliced*
2 fat	Tomatoes, seeded and chopped
1/2 c	Black olives, sliced
1	Green pepper, thinly sliced into ribs

Sauce:

1 c	Parsley without stems
3	Green onions, sliced
1/3 c	Lemon juice
1/2 Tbl	Dijon mustard
1 tsp	Honey and onion powder
2 Tbl	Tofunaise or eggless light mayo
	Cracked pepper

1) Cook rotellis al dente—rinse and drain.
2) Put vegetables in large bowl, add pasta.
3) Blend sauce in blender till smooth, pour over pasta. Stir together.

Mushrooms can be simmered in 1 tsp olive oil and garlic before adding to pasta.

Serves 4-6

Tortellinis with Seasonal Vegetables

1 (16 oz) pk	Tortellinis
2	Zucchinis, shredded
1/2 lg	Onion
1/2 sm	Eggplant, cubed
2 c	Sliced mushrooms
2	Tomatoes, seeded, chopped
2	Garlic cloves, pressed
1	Lemon, juiced
1/4 c	Liquid aminos
2 Tbl	Pinenuts, toasted
1 Tbl	Red wine and 1 Tbl water
	Cracked pepper
2 Tbl ea	Olive oil optional, red wine vinegar

1) Cook tortellinis till tender, rinse and drain.
2) Sauté garlic in wine, lemon and water, add mushrooms, eggplant, and chopped onion and aminos. When tender put into large bowl.
3) Toss everything together—adjust seasonings.

Pesto Pasta Salad

This is rich, but delicious. It makes a pretty summer meal.

1 lb	Pasta (tortellinis, rotellis or elbows)
1/4 c	Pesto, see recipe
1	Red bell pepper, sliced
1	Yellow bell pepper, sliced
1 c	Walnuts or pecans, toasted
1/4 c	Rice vinegar or lime juice

1) Cook pasta al dente, mix vinegar with pesto.
2) Stir everything together, chill.

Hiziki & Ramen Sea Noodle Salad

*Seaweed and oriental noodles are nestled amongst
salad and spices.*

1 pk	Ramen or soba (1/2 lb.)
	Several Kale leaves
1	Small head cabbage, shredded
1/2 c	Hiziki (soak in 3/4 c water for 15 min., drain)
3	Green onions, minced
1 tsp	Ginger roots, minced
1	Carrot, grated
dash	Cayenne

Sauce:

3 Tbl	Tamari
2 tsp	Toasted sesame oil
3 Tbl	Rice vinegar
2 Tbl	Brown sesame seeds

1) Cook soba, when al dente add kale and cabbage to water. Cover
for a couple of minutes, then drain and rinse (or save stock for
a soup).

2) Prepare hiziki, blend sauce, and toss everything together.

Serve with low-cal ginger dressing on side if desired. Garnish
with curly endive and a flower.

Thai-bright Salad

2 oz	Bean thread noodles
2	Carrots
1/2	Jicama
1 Tbl	Lime juice and grated skin
2 Tbl	Rice vinegar
1 Tbl	Rice syrup
1/4 c	Torn mint leaves (loose pack)
1/4 c	Cilantro leaves (loose pack)
dash	Red chile flakes, sesame oil and tamari
2 Tbl	Minced peanuts

1) Soak noodles in boiling water for 10 minutes until al dente.
2) Shred carrots and dice jicama.
3) Mix next 3 ingredients, pour over veggies in bowl.
4) Toss all together, smile.

Simple Soba Salad

1 (6 oz) pk	Soba (buckwheat) noodles
5 dried	Shiitake mushrooms
3 1/2 Tbl	Tamari
2 Tbl	Sesame oil, cold pressed
2 Tbl	Rice vinegar
1 Tbl	Honey
1 Tbl	Hot pepper oil—(toasted sesame fire oil)
6	Scallions, minced
2 Tbl	Black sesame seeds

1) Cook soba according to directions on pack, or till al dente.
2) Toss them in a large bowl with rest of ingredients.
3) Decorate with carrot stars if desired—cut "V" shapes out of carrot lengthwise, then slice into "stars."

Marinated Tofu in Soba Noodles

This is a cross between a soup and a salad and is a wonderful light meal.

Firm tofu cut in 1/2″ thick slices (figure a 2 oz slice per serving)
Soba noodles, cooked and drained
Chopped cilantro leaves
Cherry tomatoes
Sprouts (radish, alfalfa and clover)
Toasted sesame seeds

Marinade:
1/4 c	**Mirin cooking sake**
1/4 c	**Soy sauce**
1 tsp	**Ginger, freshly minced**
	Cayenne

1) Stir marinade together and spoon over tofu, let sit for as long as you can, it's still great if you don't have any time to wait.
2) Put tofu in a toaster oven and broil it for 10 minutes or so.
3) Put noodles in individual deep bowls.
4) Lay tofu and it's sizzling juices on top, then garnish with salad goodies.

Serve with a Japanese spoon and chopsticks.

Pasta Oriental

1 lb	Fusilli pasta
1/2 hd	Cabbage, shredded thickly (1/4-1/2" strips)
1/2 lg	Onion
10	Shiitake mushrooms (soak in water 15 minutes if dried, remove stems)
1 15 oz.can	Palm hearts, sliced
1 small can	Water chestnuts, quartered
1 can	Baby corns
1	Red pepper thinly sliced

Sauté sauce for mushrooms and onions:

2 Tbl ea.	Water and Tamari
1 Tbl ea.	Honey, Mirin and minced ginger root
dash	Cayenne and toasted sesame oil

1) Cook pasta till al dente, turn off heat then add cabbage to water for a few minutes, drain and rinse.
2) Slice mushrooms and onion, simmer in saute sauce for 10 minutes, covered on low heat.
3) Toss all together in big bowl with:

3	Garlic cloves, pressed
1/2	Lemon, juiced
	Tamari to taste

Garnish top with cilantro leaves and sesame seeds.

Tropical Tempeh Salad
in Canteloupe Shells

2	**Small canteloupes**
1/2 pkg	**Tempeh, chopped (4 oz.)**
1/2	**Lemon, juiced**
2 Tbl	**Coconut shreds**
1 tsp	**Curry powder**
1 lg	**Spoonful soy yogurt**
	Liquid aminos

1) Marinate tempeh 1 hour in aminos, then steam 15 min.
2) Slice melons in half, seed them and scoop out flesh in small balls or chunks. Slice off bottom of each half of melon so it can sit correctly.
3) Put melon balls in a bowl with rest of ingredients, toss.
4) Adjust seasonings and fill up melon bowls, garnish with chives, lemon twists, raisins, or toasted nuts.

SALAD DRESSINGS

Purifying = Dressings on the light side with vegetables and juices
Fortifying = Heartier dressings using nuts, tofu, tofumayo, vinegars
or oils.
Sweet = Sauces for fruit or desserts.

SALAD DRESSINGS

The right salad dressing can push your taste buds right into a sublime realm of ecstasy, boost nutrition and complete the protein of your favorite salad.

I've provided a broad range of healthy tastes in these dressings; those prepared with tofu, with sprouted or toasted nuts and seeds, without any oils or fats using all vegetables and juices, and a few light vinaigrettes using some pure virgin oils.

Salad dressings are fun and easy to make, and so much tastier and better for you than the store bought ones.

Treat yourself special while preparing food, keep a gardenia in
a vase to fill up the air with heaven.

Golden Temple Dressing

These are purifying and delicious!

1 c	Fresh carrot juice
1	Garlic clove
1/4 med	Avocado*
1/2	Lemon, juiced
	Small piece ginger

Blend till smooth.

Rose Temple Dressing

1 c	Beet juice
1	Garlic clove
1/4 med	Avocado
1/2	Lemon, juiced
	Ginger

Blend till smooth.

*Avocados are very high in fat, so use them sparingly.

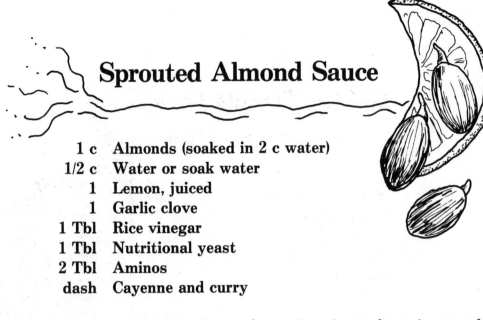

Sprouted Almond Sauce

1 c	Almonds (soaked in 2 c water)
1/2 c	Water or soak water
1	Lemon, juiced
1	Garlic clove
1 Tbl	Rice vinegar
1 Tbl	Nutritional yeast
2 Tbl	Aminos
dash	Cayenne and curry

1) Soak almonds overnight to release vitamins and nutrients and to increase their digestability.
2) Blend almonds in blender till smooth; add rest and blend, add water if necessary.

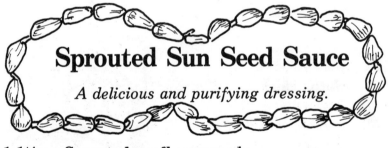

Sprouted Sun Seed Sauce

A delicious and purifying dressing.

1 1/4 c	Sprouted sunflower seeds
4	Garlic cloves
1/4 c	Lemon juice
2 Tbl	Aminos
1 c	Water or soak water
dash	Cayenne

1) Put all in blender, add water last, thin to desired consistency. Using soak water from sunseed sprouts will add more vitamins and minerals (see sprouting section).
2) Blend till smooth, chill.

Divine over steamed vegetables, or in a pita sandwich.

Low-cal Garlic Herb

Use as a marinade for vegetables.

2 c	Water
1/4 tsp	Agar flakes
5 Tbl	Cider or red wine vinegar
1 1/2 Tbl	Garlic, chopped
2	Green onions
2 tsp	Onion powder
1 tsp	Coriander, basil, oregano
1/2 tsp	Cracked black pepper
1 tsp	Barley malt syrup or honey

1) Dissolve agar in water then transfer pot to high flame. Bring to boil for 1 min. then remove and pour into blender.
2) Add rest of ingredients, blend and refrigerate.

Orange Miso Dressing

Great on cabbage slaws and chilled bean salads.

1 c	Orange juice
3 Tbl	Mellow white miso
3 sm	Garlic cloves
1 Tbl	Honey or maple syrup
1 Tbl	Rice vinegar

Blend till smooth.

Ginger Sesame Marinade

2c   Water
1/2 tsp   Agar flakes
6 Tbl   Rice vinegar
2 Tbl   Ginger, chopped
1/4 c   Honey
2 Tbl   Tamari
2 Tbl   Brown sesame seeds
    Few drops sesame oil toasted

1)   In a small sauce pan soak agar in in water till it dissolves, bring to boil, remove from heat and pour it into a blender.
2)   Add vinegar and ginger, blend well and strain off fibers.
3)   Add rest of ingredients to blender, continue blending then refrigerate.

Avocado Sauce

Great on coleslaw and salads, but rich.

1   Avocado
1/4 c   Cilantro leaves, packed
2   Garlic cloves
1/4 c   Lemon juice
1 Tbl   Liquid aminos
1/2 tsp   Cumin
dash   Cayenne
1 1/4 c   Water

Blend in blender till soft and silky.

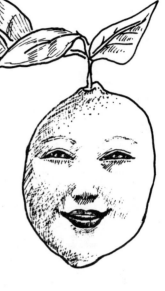

Alive Salad Sauce

This is purifying and zippy.

2	Lemons, juiced
1	Garlic clove
1 Tbl	Ginger, freshly chopped
2 Tbl	Aminos
1 1/2 Tbl	Nutritional yeast
1 Tbl	Tahini
1 tsp	Honey or barley malt syrup

Blend.

Tomato Tahini

1 1/2 c	Tomato juice
1/2	Lemon, juiced
2	Garlic cloves
1	Jalapeño (seed first if you don't like "hot")
1 1/2 Tbl	Tahini
1 Tbl	Nutritional yeast
1/2 Tbl	Aminos
	Cracked pepper
2 Tbl	Onion, chopped

Blend all till smooth and creamy, adjust seasonings to taste.

24 Carrot Sauce

Delicious! One of my favorites.

1 c	Carrot juice
1/2	Lemon, juiced
1/4 c	Soft tofu
1 lg	Spoonful egglessmayo or soymayo
2	Garlic cloves, pressed
1/2 tsp	Dill weed
2 Tbl	Balsamic vinegar
	Tamari and cayenne to taste

Blend in blender till smooth.

Honey Mustard Vinaigrette

A tart and spicy low-cal vinaigrette, great over coleslaws.

1/2 c	Red wine vinegar
2 Tbl	Tarragon mustard
2 Tbl	Lemon juice
2 Tbl	Honey

Blend.

Spicy Thousand Island

Adds zest and a beautiful color to salads.

1/2 c	Natural ketchup mixed with 1/2 c water or more
1/2 c	Eggless mayo or tofunaise
2 Tbl	Salsa
1 1/2	Lemons, juiced (approx. 1/4 c)
2	Garlic cloves, chopped

Blend in blender till creamy.

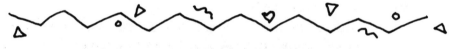

Almond Ginger Sauce

Great as a dip or salad dressing, on potatoes or steamed veggies.
Highly nutritious.

1 c	Almonds, soaked (soak in purified water overnight) yields 1 1/2c almonds
1/4 c	Almonds, roasted
2 c	Broth (or soaked water)
2	Garlic cloves
1 Tbl	Ginger, freshly chopped
1 Tbl	Soy sauce
2 Tbl	Lemon juice
1/8 tsp	Cayenne (or to taste)

Blend till smooth.

Jalapeño Dill Creme

*Sesame tahini and soft tofu are blended to form a creamy base
for this exciting sauce.*

1 c	Soft tofu
1 Tbl	Tahini
1	Jalapeño (seeded if you don't like hot)
1 tsp	Dill weed
1	Garlic clove
1 Tbl	Lemon juice
dash	Tamari to taste
	(Add a couple of drops of toasted sesame oil if a more prominant sesame taste is desired)

1) Blend in blender till soft and silky.
2) Garnish with toasted sesame seeds, dill or lemon slivers.

Use as a sauce for rice or vegetables, salad dressing or dip.

Salsa Creme

A spicy creamy salad dressing.

1/4 c	Hot fresh salsa
1/2 c	Tofu crumbled
1	Juicy lemon or lime
1 Tbl	Soy yogurt
1/2 Tbl	Aminos
1/2 tsp	Honey

Blend till creamy.

Yogurt Tahini

Delicious as a dressing, a sauce for falafel sandwiches, or over pasta.

8 oz.	Soy yogurt
3 Tbl	Tahini
1	Lemon, juiced
2	Garlic cloves
1 Tbl	Mellow white miso
	Fresh parsley leaves
	Cracked black pepper

Blend everything.

Tofu Sesame Sauce

1 c	Soft tofu
1 Tbl	Tahini
1/2	Lemon, juiced (approx. 3 Tbl)
2 Tbl	Toasted sesame seeds
2 Tbl	Chopped onion (or 2 tsp powder)
1	Garlic clove, pressed
1/2 tsp	Honey
2 tsp	Tamari
1/4 c	Water

1) Blend tofu and tahini and lemon juice in Blender.
2) Slowly add water and rest of ingredients.
3) Blend till smooth.

Chile Peanut Sauce

Try over a Mexican salad or coleslaw featuring bell peppers, jicama, cabbage and carrots; yields 1 1/4 c.

1 c	Tomato juice
1 Tbl	Peanut butter
3/4 tsp	Chile powder
1 Tbl	Lemon juice
1	Garlic clove
dash	Cayenne

1) Blend till smooth.
2) Tomato juice can be replaced with 3 Tbl natural ketchup diluted with 3/4 c water.

Italian Herbal Vinaigrette

Nutritious spirulina turns this vinaigrette green.

1/4 c	Olive oil, cold, pressed
1/4 c	Lemon juice
1/4 c	Apple cider vinegar
1/4 c	Water
2 Tbl	Sun seeds or pinenuts, toasted
2 Tbl	Soy Parmesan cheese
1 tsp	Spirulina
1/2 tsp	Oregano and basil
2	Garlic cloves
1/4 tsp	Black pepper
dash	Sea salt

Blend till smooth. Freshly toasted sun seeds have the best flavor.

Spinach Dressing

1/2 bunch	Spinach, steamed tender
1/8 c	Sun seeds, toasted
2	Garlic cloves, pressed
1/2	Lemon, juiced
1/3	Jalapeño, minced
1 tsp	Onion powder
	Water to thin, tamari to taste

Put all into a blender, blend till smooth and creamy.

Toasted Lime Dressing

Delicious—especially nice on spinach salads with shredded red cabbage, radish sprouts and cucumbers.

1/2 c	Tofu, crumbled
1/4 c	Sunflower seeds
1/2 c	Water
3	Green onions
3	Limes
3 Tbl	Rice vinegar
1	Garlic clove
1 Tbl	Eggless mayo
1 Tbl	Aminos

1) Toast sun seeds till light brown.
2) Course chop onions, juice limes
3) Blend everything till smooth in blender.

Creamy Dill

A high protein, low calorie, delicious green dressing.

1 c	Tofu (soft or silken)
2 Tbl	Tofunaise or mayo
1/4 c	Lemon juice, fresh
1 tsp	Onion powder
1/4 c	Fresh dill leaves
2 Tbl	Wine vinegar
1 Tbl	Apple juice
2 Tbl	Pinenuts or sunflower seed, toasted

Blend smooth and chill.

Yogurtnaise

A zesty soy yogurt mayo.

1/2	Lemon, juiced (or 3 Tbl)
1/2 c	Soy yogurt
2 Tbl	Herb red wine vinegar or apple cider vinegar
1	Garlic clove, pressed
dash	Cayenne and aminos

Blend till smooth.

Easy Sweet Yogurt Sauce

Serve over fruit, or spice cake.

1 c	Soy yogurt
1 tsp	Vanilla
2 Tbl	Honey
2 Tbl	Lemon juice
	Few drops maple extract
	Cinnamon as garnish

Stir above ingredients in a small bowl and chill.

Peanut Paradise

2 Tbl	Peanut butter
2 oz	Soft tofu
1/4 c	Water
1 Tbl	Honey
1/2	Banana
	Apple juice or soymilk to thin

Blend, adding juice to desired thickness. Can be used as a delicious shake, adding more apple juice and crushed ice.

Coco Lime Fruit Glaze

A very refreshing sauce for fruit salads.

1/4 c   Lime, juiced
2 Tbl   Honey
2 Tbl   Thick coconut milk

Whisk together.

Sauce of Angels

Delicious with cakes or over fruit gels.

1 c   Cottage tofu
1/4 c   Fructose
1 tsp   Vanilla

Blend in blender till smooth.

Fruity Tofu Creme Sauce

Serve on the side with your fruit salads.

1 pk   Silken tofu
3 Tbl   Lemon juice
4 Tbl   Natural fruit syrup (raspberry or strawberry)
1/2 tsp   Vanilla
1/2 tsp   Lemon peel, grated
1/3 c   Orange juice
1 tsp   Poppy seeds

Puree until smooth.

FUN FOODS

FUN FOODS

Healthy Snacks and appetite teasers are *fun* foods. The kind of thing you serve at a party when everyone stands around the kitchen eating and talking, or when you curl up in bed to read, or watch a movie. These light meals have much versatility, so you can spread, dip and sprinkle anything on them that sounds good to you.

Fun foods are the perfect companion for solitary nibbling, seductive noshes for intimate twosomes, or full on party foods for large gatherings.

Whatever the occasion, these foods are fun!

Chapati Party Pizzas

A fun appetizer or party food.

Baja style:

> Whole wheat chapatis
> Grated jalapeño soy cheese
> 2   Zucchinis halved, sliced lengthwise in 1/4″thick slabs
> Roasted red bell peppers
> Fresh cilantro
> Red salsa

1) Steam zucchinis till crisp—tender.
2) Toast chapatis in oven on cookie sheet till just crisp, not brown, remove from oven.
3) Cover with grated soy cheese, zucchini strips, more soy cheese, green onions and red peppers.
4) Toast or broil till soy cheese melts—3-5 minutes.
5) Serve with salsa swirled on top and cilantro leaves.

For variations I suggest adding after soy cheese:

Italian—*Add sliced olives, marinara sauce, basil leaves, sliced tofu pups and garlic.*

Mexican—*Add avocado slices, black beans,* **Red Chile Sauce,** *p. 129.*

Thai—*Add crushed peanuts, cilantro, mint, red chili flakes, and* **Tofu Thai Peanut Sauce,** *p. 138.*

Have fun experimenting!

Potato Latkes

Dairyless, eggless potato pancakes. Serve with apple sauce and soy yogurt, marinara sauce or ketchup, or garnish with sliced tomatoes and dill.

3/4 c	Soy milk
1/2 c	Tofu, packed
3 Tbl	Flour
1 Tbl	Onion powder
2 sm	Potatoes
1/4	Onion

1) Puree tofu in blender, add soy milk.
2) Shred or grate potatoes and onion in food processor, squeeze and blot dry.
3) Put tofu and vegetable in bowl, stir together.
4) Pour mix onto hot oiled griddle and flip when brown.

Eggplant Rounds

A curry paste gets brushed on top of eggplant slices and broiled for a quick treat.

1 sm	Eggplant, sliced in rounds 1/2″ thick
1 tsp	Curry powder
1/4 tsp ea	Cumin, coriander, onion powder
1 tsp	Aminos
	Lemon juice
	Water as needed
1/2 tsp	Olive oil

1) Stir together spices to make a paste—brush on eggplants.
2) Broil for several minutes till tender.

Lo-Cal Popcorn

Mix air popped popcorn with nutritional yeast, aminos, cayenne, lemon juice and whatever spices delight you—curry is great!

Baked Tofu Rice Balls

2 c	Brown rice, cooked (or leftover)
1	Garlic clove
2/3 lb	Tofu
1 Tbl	Onion powder
1/2 c	Almonds, toasted
3 Tbl	Oat bran
	Sea salt

1) Stir together in food processor or chop till everything is evenly distributed.
2) Roll into small 1 1/2″ round balls.
   Roll into desired coating:
   Onion powder and diced onions
   Seasoned bread crumbs
3) Bake 30 minutes at 400°.

Serve with **Spicy cilantro dipping sauce** *—see recipe in sauces.*

Makes 24-30 balls

Mochi Puffs

Sold in many gourmet and natural food stores, mochi is a sweet glutinous rice formed into a flat cake. Break it apart into 2" squares and toast it until it puffs up and gets browned. A chewy delicious snack.

    1 pack   Mochi; (makes 9, 2" squares)
                  Spicy cilantro dipping sauce—see recipe p. 145

1) Preheat oven at 450°
2) Break apart mochi, place on top rack of oven, bake until toasty approx. 5-10 minutes.
3) Arrange on a serving platter, serve sauce in center.

Option: fill mochi puffs with tofu stuffing from tofu-stuffed tomato recipe.

Nori Toastitos

Nori is a perfect diet food, for it is a low calorie mineral rich "tortilla" that will hold any foods of your imagination. Have fun creating a salad and sauce smörgasbord, making sure your nori doesn't burn. It should toast to a light green color, in only seconds.

1 pack	**Nori sheets, toasted**
	Sprouts of choice (buckwheat, sunflower, alfalfa,
	Steamed carrot sticks, whole peas or other veggies
	Your favorite sauce or dressing,
	(or go traditional with wasabi paste and tamari)

1) Roll up jellyroll style and seal with water, or cut into triangle and roll up like a cone.

Have fun rolling your own!

No-oil Chips & Salsa

1 dz.	**Corn tortillas**
1 Recipe	**Salsa Fresca**

1) Toast whole tortillas on oven rack for 10-15 min. until crisp (who needs all that oil?)
2) Break apart in 1/4's and serve around a center bowl of salsa.

Bring out the **Black Bean Party Dip*** *for a real feast.*

Mexican Flag Seed Cheese Nachos

Per person

1	Corn tortilla
3 Tbl	Seed cheese
2 Tbl	Salsa
	Several black olives, sliced
	Cilantro, fresh, to garnish

1) Toast tortillas in oven a couple of minutes until crunchy.
2) Spread seed cheeese on top, pour salsa on next, garnish with olives and cilantro, olé!

Crispy Baked Wontons

A delightful party appetizer that's not fried. Serve with **Spicy Cilantro Dipping Sauce** *or* **Tofu Thai Peanut Sauce.**

Follow recipe for **Wontons in Kombu Broth***, up to step 6 until cooked al dente, strain onto a platter. Meanwhile pre-heat oven to Broil. Oil a ventilated rack (or use a non stick baking sheet) and place wontons on top. Broil until light brown, turn with tongs and broil other side.

These will take approximately 10-15 minutes on each side, keep an eye on them. Serve hot, right out of the oven.

*Recipe found on page 273

SAUCES, DIPS & CONDIMENTS

Introduction 127

SAUCES, DIPS & CONDIMENTS

What provides variety to a vegetarian's diet? Why, a sauce, of course. Any fruit, vegetable or grain can be bathed, dipped, and dressed to dazzle the diner with an endless parade of sensations. A new and exciting sauce can awaken tiresome tastebuds and bring adventure to the table.

Many people pass on sauces due to their high fat and calorie rich ingredients, so I have provided some healthy recipes that will spring board your imagination into future sauce serendipity.

Chile Roja Enchilada Sauce

*Roasted ancho or pasilla chiles, create a great and memorable sauce.
I learned to make this from the Mexi-Indians in Baja. This is my
own adaptation (they use much more oil).*

2-3 oz pk	Pasilla chiles, dried (they should be big and ruby black)
2 1/4 c	Water
1 1/2 tsp	Oregano
2 tsp	Cumin
1 sm can	Tomato paste
1/2 tsp	Sea salt
1	Garlic clove

1) Bake chiles in preheated 350° oven for 3-4 minutes, cool.
2) Remove pithy insides, stems, and seeds.
3) Put in a small pan, cover with water, bring to a boil, then simmer on low 15 minutes. Remove skin.
4) Put chile pulp into blender along with water and blend. Add other ingredients, continue blending till a smooth texture reveals.

*Yields 4c—can be frozen. Besides enchiladas, you can add this sauce
to rice or beans for a great flavor.*

Chile Verde Sauce

This delicious thick green sauce has a distinctive mellow and nutty flavor with a hot after taste.

1/2 c	Almonds
8 lg	Green California chiles (or 1 1/2 c cooked chiles)
1 med	Onion
2	Garlic cloves
1 sm	Jalapeño
2 c	Water
2 Tbl	Cilantro
2 Tbl	Aminos

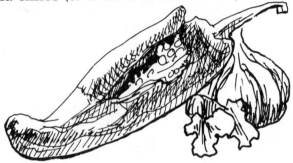

1) Toast almonds till lightly browned.
2) Toast chiles whole in oven till fragrant and both sides are blistered. Place in a plastic bag and let cool, then seed and skin them.
3) Sauté chopped onion and jalapeños in 2 Tbl aminos till tender approx. 5 minutes. Stir occasionally.
4) Put almonds, chiles, and rest of ingredients into a food processor or blender and puree till smooth.
5) Return to saucepan and simmer for 10 more minutes.

Serve with **Chile Verde Enchiladas, Tomatillo Enchilada Casserole, Tofu Chilaquiles.** *Or sauté tofu or tempeh slices in this sauce as a main dish and serve over rice, with beans, and tortillas or over pasta. Also delicious over burritos and baked.*

*Note, it will be rather hot if all seeds are not removed.

Tomato Vegetable Cream Sauce

A heavenly sauce, serve over tortellinis or pasta of your choice.

1/2 c ea.	Onion, carrot, celery
3 Tbl	White wine
2 1/2 c	Italian tomatoes with juice
6 lg	Basil leaves, fresh
1 tsp	Vegetable salt substitute and pepper
1/2 c	Soy milk

1) Mince vegetables in food processor.
2) Sauté them in a large skillet in wine.
3) Add tomatoes, basil and spices simmer 45 minutes stirring now and then with a wooden spoon.
4) Puree it in a food processor or blender.
5) Transfer back to skillet, heat up, add soy milk stir till blended and serve over pasta.

Mushroom Gravy

Very easy and full of flavor.

1 pkg	Natural mushroom soup mix
1 1/4 c	Soy milk
1/4 c	Wine
1	Garlic clove, pressed
1/2 Tbl	Aminos
	Water as needed

1) In small saucepan sauté garlic in aminos 3-4 minutes.
2) Add rest of ingredients, stir well with a whisk till bubbling, reduce heat, then simmer 10-15 minutes, stir occasionally.

Eggplant Sauce

This is much more interesting than a typical marinara sauce, serve with fresh pasta, and a large crisp salad.

1	Eggplant
1	Onion
2	Garlic cloves
28oz can	Tomatoes, crushed
6oz. can	Tomato paste and water to thin
1/4 c	Red wine
1 tsp (ea.)	Oregano and basil
1/2 tsp (ea.)	Crushed red pepper and fennel seeds
1/2 tsp	Sea salt
1 Tbl	Lemon juice or 1 lemon wedge
1 Tbl	Honey

1) Skin and dice eggplant, chop onion.
2) Press garlic into red wine, sauté in deep skillet.
3) Add eggplant, onion, continue stirring 5 min. or so.
4) Add tomatoes, paste, water and rest of ingredients.
5) Cook on low, covered for 2 hrs. Stir occasionally.

For a meaty sauce add:
Crumbled tempeh marinated in 1 Tbl aminos for 1 hr. Broil till crispy or sauté in a bit of olive oil. Then add to sauce.

Spinach Mint Sauce

1/4 c	Water
5 oz	Spinach, steamed (fresh or frozen)
1 1/2 c	Mint leaves
3	Garlic cloves
1 Tbl	Lemon juice
1/2	Serrano chile (seeded)
1 Tbl	Soy milk
1 Tbl	Aminos
	Water to thin, approx. 3/4 c

1) Sauté garlic, chile and mint in lemon juice and 1/4 c water for 5 minutes.
2) Transfer to blender and add aminos, steamed spinach, soy milk and water to thin (note, for a creamier sauce use all soy milk).
3) Blend till creamy.

Spinach Tomato Sauce

3	Tomatoes
1/2	Onion
1 bunch	Spinach
1/4 c	Water
1 Tbl	Lemon juice
2	Garlic cloves
1/4 tsp ea.	Red pepper flakes and nutmeg
1 Tbl	Aminos
1 tsp	Honey

1) Sauté first three ingredients in water till tender.
2) Puree them in food processor or blender.
3) Add rest of ingredients.
4) Transfer to a saucepan and and heat gently before serving.
5) Add soy milk for a thicker sauce.

Serve over noodles or soba.

Tofu Creme Sauce

This sauce is great on steamed broccoli or as a dip for artichokes.

1/2 lb	Tofu
1/4 c	Safflower oil
1	Lemon, juiced
2 tsp	Fructose or honey
1/2 tsp ea.	Black pepper, sea salt and mustard powder
Dash	Cayenne and nutmeg

Blend till creamy, yields 1 3/4 c sauce.

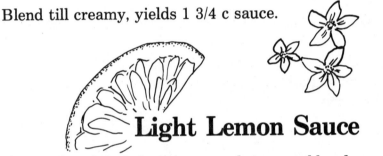

Light Lemon Sauce

A silky low calorie lemon sauce that resembles drawn butter, yet there is no dairy or fat in it. Excellent over asparagus, broccoli, artichokes or spinach.

2 c	Bouillon, water or stock
1/4 c	Lemon juice and some grated rind if it's organic
1/4 tsp	Turmeric
2 Tbl	Aminos
1 1/2 Tbl	Arrowroot powder
2	Garlic cloves, pressed
1/2 tsp	Fructose (or honey)
1 1/2 Tbl	Nutritional yeast
	Black pepper or cayenne to taste

1) Heat water in a heavy pot.
2) Mix arrowroot with some cold water and add to pot.
3) Add rest of ingredients, stirring continuously until it thickens.
4) Adjust seasonings. (cooks quickly)

Serve warm.

 Pinenut Bechamel Sauce

This is a delicious sauce. Pour over veggies, rice, pasta, or use in casseroles.

1/2 c	Pinenuts
1/4 c	Sunflower seeds
2/3 c	Onion, chopped
3	Garlic cloves, pressed
1 tbl	Red wine
1 tbl	Water
1 pkg	Silken soft tofu (10 oz.)
1 c	Soy Milk
2 tsp	Lemon juice
1 tbl	Liquid aminos (or dash of sea salt)
	Saffron (a few grains)
	Red Chili flakes
1 tsp	Coriander powder
	Cayenne (a dash)

1) Toast pinenuts and sunflower seeds until golden. Reserve 1 tbl seeds for garnish.
2) Sauté chopped onion, and garlic cloves. Add red wine and water mixture.
3) Mash tofu and onion together with saffron, fennel seeds, chili flakes and coriander.
4) Put in blender with seeds and add dash of cayenne, soy milk, lemon juice and sea salt.

Cashew Pepper Gravy

A hearty roasted flavor pervades this creamy oil-less, dairy-less gravy.
Serve over oven roasted vegetables and grains.

1	Onion, chopped
1	Lemon, juiced
1 c	Cashew pieces
2 tsp	Arrowroot powder
2 c	Water mixed with;
1 Tbl	Mineral Bouillon
1 tsp	Onion powder
1 tsp	Jalapeño, roasted and diced
	Dash of seasalt, cracked black pepper and nutmeg

1) Sauté onion in lemon juice in skillet until tender.
2) Toast cashews in oven until light brown, toast jalapeño pepper until skin bubbles.
3) Peel, seed and chop jalapeño, put in blender or food processor with nuts and onion and some water—puree.
4) Mix arrowroot with 1/4 c water. Put into sauce pan and heat up with rest of mixtures. Stir until sauce thickens. Adjust spices.

Garnish with grated lemon peel.

Toasted Pecan Sauce

A roasted nutty gravy that suits steamed vegetables or noodles.

1/2 c	Pecans
1 pk	Silken tofu (10.5 oz.)
1	Onion
1	Celery rib and leaves
1 Tbl	Cooking sherry
1 Tbl	Lemon juice
1	Garlic clove
	Several parsley sprigs
	Tamari to taste
	Water to thin

1) Toast pecans lightly, then put in food processor to grind finely, add tofu.
2) Chop vegetables, heat lemon juice and sherry in heavy skillet, then add vegetables stirring till they soften on low heat.
3) Add veggies, garlic, parsley and liquids to processor, puree till smooth, adding water or broth.
4) Transfer to medium pot and heat gently before serving.

Tofu Thai Peanut Sauce

Serve as a sauce over soba noodles or as a dip for broiled tempeh, eggrolls, rice or steamed vegetables.

10.5 oz pk	Silken tofu
4 Tbl	Peanuts, crushed or peanut butter
1 lg	Garlic clove
1 Tbl ea.	Ginger, freshly chopped, and lime juice
1/4 c	Coconut milk
1/2 Tbl	Soy sauce
1	Green onion
	Few mint and cilantro leaves
	Dash of red chili flakes
	Water to thin

Blend till smooth and chill.

Indian Coconut Sauce

1 c	Coconut Milk (or blend 1 1/2c coconut with 1c water and strain)
2 Tbl	Peanut butter
1 Tbl	Ginger, freshly chopped
1 Tbl	Curry, see recipe
1 tsp	Turmeric
1/4 c	Cilantro leaves loosely packed
1/2 c	Pineapple juice
1 tsp	Agar

1) Blend first 6 ingredients in small bowl.
2) Dissolve agar in pineapple juice—heat until boiling. Turn off and blend other ingredients into it.
3) Heat until warm. Serve over grains.

Satin Sauce

A gently spiced serene sauce with hints of orange, apricot and cardamon. Fresh spices are the key to a rich flavor.

1 c	Silken or soft tofu
2 c	Water
4 tsp	Arrowroot
2 Tbl	Aminos
1 Tbl	Onion powder
1/2 c	Orange juice, fresh squeezed
3/4 tsp ea.	Cardamon and nutmeg
2	Garlic cloves
2 Tbl	Apricot or peach preserves, unsweetened
2 Tbl	White wine
	Dash of curry powder
2 tsp	Onion powder

1) Blend items in blender.
2) Transfer to a medium sized enamel pot and heat gently, stir well on low.

Makes 4 cups

Green Sauce

A Peruvian sauce using tofu, fresh mint, garlic and fresh cilantro.
Excellent on steamed veggies, over pasta, or as a dip.

8 oz	Soft tofu
1/3 c	Cilantro, chopped
1/4 c	Mint, chopped
4	Garlic cloves
1 Tbl	Aminos
1/4 c	Water (or to thin)
	Cayenne to taste

Blend everything well in a blender. *Serves 2-4*

Sprouted Garbanzo Sauce

Makes a great pureed soup, and a warm sauce for rice and grains.

1 c	Garbanzos
1	Bell pepper
1	Onion
3	Garlic cloves
1/2	Lemon juice
1 Tbl	Olive oil
1/4 c	Torn cilantro leaves
	Sea salt and Cayenne to taste

1) Soak garbanzos overnight, rinse in mornings and evenings for 2-4 days, until sprouts appear.
2) Put garbanzos in a pot, cover with water, bring to boil then simmer 20 minutes.
3) Chop onions and peppers, mince garlic, add to pot, cook another 30 minutes or until tender.
4) Transfer to blender, add other ingredients, and more water as needed.

Wok Glaze

This is a truly great glaze over any vegetable stir-fry.

1/2 c	Pineapple juice
1/4 c	Mirin (cooking sake)
1 Tbl	Arrowroot, whisked with 2 Tbl cool water
1 Tbl	Tamari
2 lg	Ginger chunks (approx. 1″ square)
2	Garlic cloves
	Orange wedge squeezed in

1) In a small saucepan, heat arrowroot mixture, stirring 2 minutes.
2) Add juice, mirin, tamari, heat and stir till thick—turn off heat.
3) Press ginger through garlic press into pan, press in garlic and add orange squeeze.
4) Heat slightly before pouring over woked vegetables.

Add dash of red chili flakes and toasted sesame seeds over vegetables.

Curried Peanut Sauce

Great over squash and rice.

1/4 lb	Tofu (1/2 c)
1/4 c	Peanut butter
1/2 tsp	Curry powder
1 tsp	Onion powder
1/2 c	Water (or soy milk for richer sauce)
1/8 tsp	Cayenne
	Turmeric for extra golden color

Blend in blender, heat before serving.

Black Bean Sauce

Try over woked wild mushrooms and roll up in (mu-shu) pancakes, or over rice or squash.

1 1/4 c	Cooked Black Beans
3	Garlic cloves
1 Tbl	Ginger root, chopped (fresh)
2 Tbl	Aminos
1/2 Tbl	Rice vinegar
1/3 c	Water or stock
	Cayenne to taste

Puree in blender.

For a heartier taste stir in 1/4 c shredded soy cheese and heat before serving. Garnish with minced chives.

Meximato Sauce

*Serve over **Chile Rellenos** or any other dish longing for a nicely spiced red sauce.*

1 (8oz) can	Tomato sauce
1	Tomato seeded and chopped
1/4	Onion, chopped
1/2 tsp ea.	Oregano, cumin and chili powder
1/2	Lemon, juiced
1	Garlic clove

1) Sauté tomatoes, onions, garlic in lemon juice on low.
2) Stir constantly, add a little water or broth if necessary.
3) Stir in tomato sauce and simmer with spices 15 minutes or so.

Cactus Salsa

A medium-hot versatile green sauce, good hot or cold. Canned, it also makes a nice gift. Many ingredients are found at farmers markets or in the Mexican section at the grocers.

7	Anaheim Chiles
3	Jalapeño peppers
1	Onion, chopped
2 c	Cactus, chopped
1 c	Cilantro leaves
1 1/2 c	Tomatillos, chopped
2	Garlic cloves
1	Lemon, juiced
1 c	Water
1/2 Tbl	Arrowroot powder (mixed with a bit of water)
2 Tbl	Aminos
1 Tbl	Honey
	Cumin to taste

1) Sauté onion, cactus and tomatillos in lemon juice until tender.
2) Toast chiles in oven until skin blisters, seed, peel and chop; put into food processor with garlic and sauteed vegetables, pulse chop until chunky-pureed. Add rest of ingredients.
3) Transfer to pot, heat gently, stirring often 10-15 minutes. Chill.

Salsa Fresca

Serve with tortilla chips or as a condiment with all sorts of foods.

9-12	Tomatoes
1/2	Red onion
1/2	Yellow onion
4	Jalapeños, seeded
1 c	Cilantro leaves
2 Tbl	Vinegar
4	Garlic cloves
1/2 tsp	Sea salt
1/2 tsp	Cumin powder

1) Seed and chop tomatoes, finely chop onions and cilantro, mince jalapeños and put into a bowl.
2) Add other ingredients, toss and chill.

Note: wear rubber gloves while handling the jalapeños or they will burn your fingers.

Pineapple Salsa

A delightful tropical salsa, serve over broiled tempeh or tofu.

2 c	Pineapple chunks
1/2 c	Onion, minced
1/4 c	Cilantro leaves
1/2	Lemon, juiced
2	Jalapeños, seeded
1	Garlic clove, pressed
2 Tbl	Pimentos and crumbled oregano

1) Press garlic and 1 jalapeño thru press, thinly slice second jalapeño.
2) Put all ingredients into a medium bowl, toss.

Spicy Cilantro Dipping Sauce

A thin and spicy sauce perfect for dipping mochi puffs, rice balls or on any grain that yearns for a jazzy companion.

2 Tbl	Tamari
1 Tbl	Mirin
1/4 c	Rice vinegar
1 Tbl	Fresh cilantro leaves, torn, loose pack
1/4 tsp	Red chile flakes
1/2 tsp. ea	Fresh ginger and jalapeño pepper, minced

Stir all together, refrigerate.

Makes 1/2 cup.

Party Black Bean Dip

2 c	Cooked black beans
1 c	Grated Soy jalapeño cheese
2	Garlic cloves
4	Green onions, minced
1/2 tsp	Sea salt
2 tsp	Cumin
	Dash of cayenne
	Garnish with cilantro leaves

Stir well, serve warm with crisp tortilla chips and salsa.

Hummus

16oz can	Garbanzos
1/4 c	Parsley, freshly chopped
2 Tbl	Olive oil
3	Garlic cloves
1/4 c	Water or as needed
1	Lemon juiced
1 tsp	Aminos
	Cracked pepper to taste
	Paprika as garnish

Blend till smooth, stopping blender and stirring a few times if necessary.

Serve in pretty bowl with thin lemon slivers, parsley, paprika sprinkles, and, of course, pita triangles warmed.

Tofu Basil Dip

10.5 oz pack	Silken tofu
2 lg	Garlic cloves
1/4	Red onion
2	Basil sprigs (leaves only)
1	Tomato, seeded and chopped
1 Tbl	Onion powder
1	Lemon or lime juiced (approx. 3 Tbl)
1 Tbl	Aminos
	Cayenne

Blend till smooth and creamy, add water if necessary.

Zucchini Dip

2 c	Chopped zucchinis, steamed till tender
2	Garlic cloves
1	Jalapeño
1 Tbl	Mayo (tofu—eggless, your choice)
1/2 tsp ea.	Coriander powder and tamari
1/2	Avocado
1 tsp	Onion powder

1) Put zucchinis in food processor or blender.
2) Press garlic and jalapeño through garlic press.
3) Blend in rest of ingredients—chill.

Red Onion Pickles

*Sweet, pink, and crunchy, the marinade softens the bite of the onion
and makes for a nice condiment.*

3	Red onions
1/3 c	Lemon juice

Mix together and refrigerate overnight.

Silken Veggie Dip

*A low calorie, high protein, all purpose dip for vegetables,
as a salad topping or alternative to "hummus." This has a crunch
from peanuts and chopped veggies along with a spicyness from garlic
and ginger.*

10.5 oz	Silken tofu, firm
1/2	Carrot
1/2	Sour pickle
2	Garlic cloves
1 tsp ea	Ginger juice, aminos, lemon juice
1 Tbl	Roasted peanuts
	Dash of curry, coriander, cayenne, onion powders

1) Pulse chop veggies in food processor, scrape down.
2) Add tofu and spices, pulse chop just until blended.

Sprinkle gomasio, cayenne or peanuts on as a garnish.

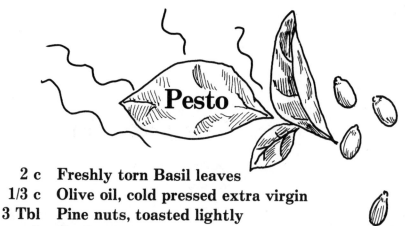

Pesto

2 c   Freshly torn Basil leaves
1/3 c Olive oil, cold pressed extra virgin
3 Tbl Pine nuts, toasted lightly
2   Garlic cloves
1/2 c Soy Parmesan cheese
1/2 tsp Sea salt

1) Put everything in blender except soy cheese, blend till smooth.
2) Stir soy cheese in by hand for an interesting texture. This can be kept frozen for several months.

Tofu Pecan Paté

Also wonderful as a vegetable dip, simply add more water.

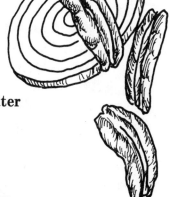

1   Handful of parsley
1/2 c   Soft tofu
1 c   Pecans
1/2   Onion
1   Garlic clove
1 Tbl   Kuzu, dissolved in 1 Tbl cold water
2 tsp ea. Cider vinegar and soy sauce
         Cayenne
1/2 Tbl Hot water if necessary

1) Toast pecans in broiler till golden brown.
2) Put them in a food processor, finely grind. Add tofu and rest of ingredients. Stop and scrape sides, continue till a smooth puree forms.
3) Put into a small oiled glass bowl, refrigerate.

A Silken Sour Cream-less

A sour cream substitute.

10.5 oz. pk	Silken tofu
2 Tbl	Lemon juice
1 Tbl	Honey or barley malt syrup

Blend till smooth.

Tofu Mayo

A low calorie mayonaise substitute. Yields 2 cups of delicious homemade mayo, use it everywhere you would use mayonaise— on sandwiches and as a base for dips and dressings.

1 c	Tofu (1/2 lb)
1 1/2 tsp	Egg replacer
1 tsp	Tarragon or dijon mustard
1 Tbl	Vinegar of choice
1 Tbl	Lemon juice
1/2 c	Good oil (virgin olive, safflower)
1/2 tsp	Sea salt or vegetable salt to taste

1) Put everything in blender except for oil—blend or liquify.
2) Slowly add oil in a thin stream until mayo begins to thicken.
3) To stabilize beat in 2 tsp boiling water.

You can vary the flavor by adding fresh minced herbs, garlic, lemon peel and pepper, enjoy!

Seed Cheese

A biogenic sunflower cheese that is high in vitamins and enzymes; easy to make and digest. Add fresh minced herbs, onion, garlic and aminos for a real treat. Use to stuff mushrooms, celery ribs, or cherry tomatoes, or as a spread on crackers. Blend with herbs and veggies for salad dressings.

1/2 c   **Sunflower seeds**
  1 c   **Pure water**

1) Soak seeds in water overnight, uncovered, in a glass jar.
2) Blend it all in blender until creamy (add a garlic clove if you wish), transfer back into jar.
3) Cover and let sit in a warm place (or in a pan of hot water) for 5-9 hours until separation occurs.
4) Pour mixture through a cheese cloth, let all water drain out for a firm cheese. Or, spoon out the soft cheese part on top, store in small container, refrigerate.

Spice and season as desired.

Cucumbermint Raita

A fragrant cooler for well spiced foods.

1/2	**Cucumber**
1 pt	**Soy yogurt**
1 c	**Cilantro or watercress leaves**
1/2c	**Mint leaves**
1	**Garlic clove, pressed**
1 Tbl	**Lemon juice**
1 tsp	**Vegetable salt**
	Dash of cayenne

1) Skin and seed cucumber, shred or dice.
2) Finely mince herbs.
3) Stir all together and chill.

Fig Chutney

*This spicy chutney makes a nice gift, prepare to can
in small glass jars afterwards, or freeze it.*

30	Figs, fresh (approx. 5-6 cups)
1/2 c	Raisins
1/4 c	Ginger, Freshly chopped
1/4 c	Lemon juice
2 med	Onions, chopped
1 tsp ea	Cardamon powder, cinnamon and cayenne
1/2 tsp ea	Clove, nutmeg, coriander, ground
1/4 c	Honey
1 Tbl	Cider vinegar
2 tsp	Agar flakes diluted with cool water to form a paste

1) Wash, stem and chop figs.
2) Put figs in heavy cast iron pot, heat on medium, then add onions, raisins and spices (except ginger).
3) Put ginger and lemon juice in blender and liquify—strain over figs in pot. Add agar mixture.
4) Stir, cover and cook on low about 1/2 hr.

Cajun Spice

Use for **Blackened Tofu or Tempeh,** *or in* **Cajun Sauce** *recipe,*
for great results.

1-3 tsp	**Cayenne (mild, medium, hot)**
1 1/2 tsp	**Black pepper, freshly ground**
1 1/2 tsp	**Sea salt**
2 tsp ea	**Oregano, thyme, fennel, cumin, cardamon, garlic powder, chili powder and coriander**

Whirl in blender or mix all together by hand and fill up jar to store.

Makes 2/3 cup

Dill Delight

1/4 c	**Dill weed**
1/8 c	**Onion powder**
2 Tbl	**Sesame seeds, toasted**
1/4 tsp	**Sea salt**
	Dash of cayenne

1) Crush sesame seeds in mill or grinder, add rest of herbs.
2) Store in a shaker jar.

Gomasio of the Sea

A highly nutritious seasoning containing the complete E.F.A.'s.
Use on salads or as a table top seasoning.

2 sheets	Toasted nori
1/2 c	Pumpkin seeds
1/2 c	Flax seeds

1) Gently toast nori till its still green, takes only seconds.
2) Grind seeds in a grinder or coffee/nut mill, add nori.
3) Put into an airtight container and keep refrigerated.

Spicy Sesame Gomasio

1/2 c	Flax seeds
1/4 c	Sesame seeds
1/4 c	Pumpkin seeds
1 Tbl	Onion powder
2 tsp	Chili powder blend
1/8 tsp	Sea salt and dash of cayenne

1) Grind seeds in grinder or mill, then add rest of ingredients to bowl, toss well.
2) Store in airtight container and chill.

Note: you can use walnuts, sunflower seeds, and nutritional yeast for other gomasio combinations. Experiment! Enjoy on salads and other dishes.

Master Curry

A fresh and fragrant curry powder, visit your local herb shop or Indian market for available spices.

1/2 c	Coriander seeds
10	Dry red chili pods (without seeds for a milder spice)
1 1/2 tsp ea	Mustard seeds, fenugreek seeds and black peppercorns
1 tsp	Cumin seeds
15-20	Curry leaves
3 Tbl	Turmeric powder

1) Grind larger seeds and pods first, then add powder.
2) Store into glass jars away from light.

Garam Masala

A traditional spice blend in India that is fun to make, yielding a very unique seasoning.

1/4 c ea	Cumin and coriander seeds
1 1/2 Tbl	Cardamon seeds
2	Cinnamon sticks, whole 3″ long
1 1/2 tsp	Whole cloves
3 Tbl	Black peppercorns
4	Bay leaves

1) Stir everything in a hot skillet for 1-2 minutes. Don't let anything burn.
2) Cool spices, then blend or grind.
3) Store in light proof container.

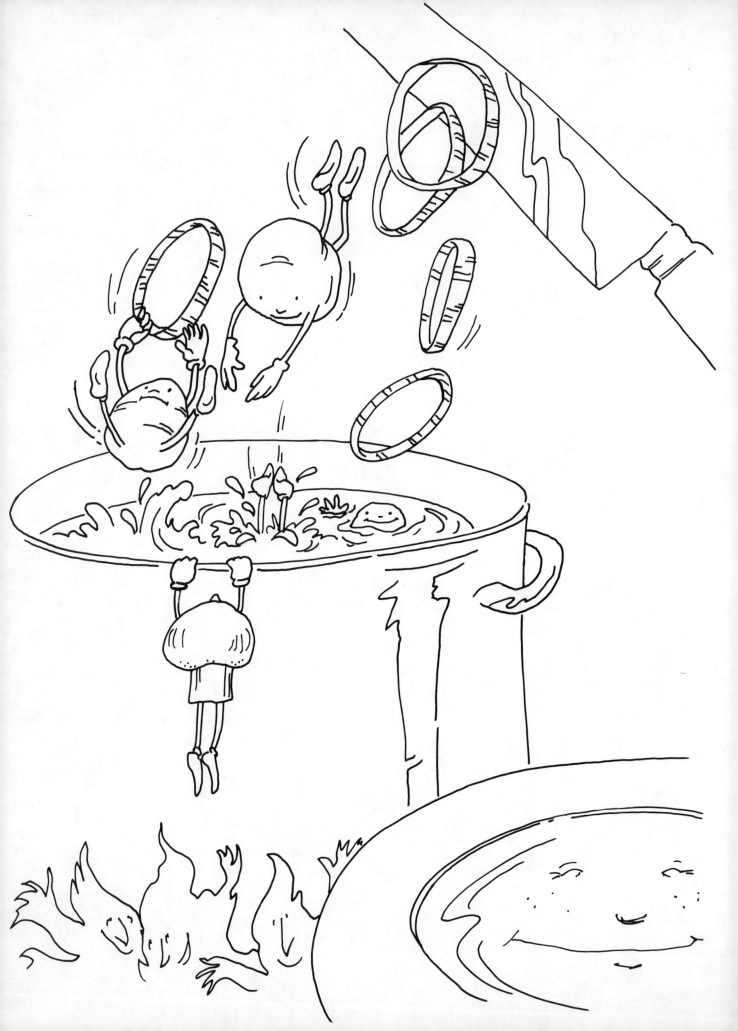

SOUPS

Purifying = Simple soups using vegetables only, very healing and easy to digest.

Creamy = Soups with a soymilk base.

Hearty = Soups fortified with tofu, grains or beans.

SOUPS

I am very fond of soup. Soup is a symphony, each ingredient singing its own song of life. I like letting time do the cooking. On chilly mornings I'll orchestrate a souphonic event, bring it to a near boil, cover and let it sit without a flame until dusk. It can be so heavenly to return home to a pot of soup, its aroma deliciously melting into the atmosphere, peacefully welcoming me home.

Ah, the seduction of soup. If only people could learn from a vegetables acceptance of being in a pot with many different fellows, yielding into one perfect gift. They give of themselves for the greater taste. Imagine a world where everyone contributes for the betterment of all. What a flavor that would be!

A word about Water

Your soups will taste better if you use purified water. A water filter system is worth the investment. It can be hooked up to your kitchen faucet, and is transportable. Most people's tap water is not very healthy, so make a change to using only purified water.

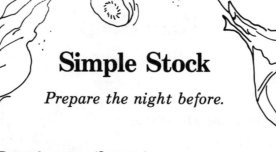

Simple Stock

Prepare the night before.

1	Pot of water (2 qrts.)
3 c	Greens, packed (Beet, chard, etc.)
1	Carrot top and leaves
1 c	Fresh parsley
1	Onion

1) Bring water to boil, add vegetables, then simmer 15-30 minutes on low.
2) Turn off and keep covered overnight.
3) Strain broth in morning.

Reducing Soup

Great hot or cold, used by itself for a couple of days takes off the weight.

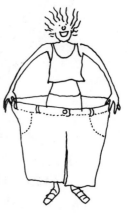

56 oz	Tomatoes, crushed (2 large size cans)
28 oz can	Water (fill up empty tomato one)
1/4 head	Green cabbage
1 head	Red cabbage
1 bunch	Celery
1	Onion
5	Garlic cloves
	Fresh or dried dill to taste

1) Chop veggies, put into large pot and fill with water.
2) Cover and bring to a near boil, simmer on low for 30 minutes or till tender. Store extra in refrigerator.

Miso Soup

Simple and satisfying.

1 qt.	Kombu broth (Dashi)
1/2	Onion
1/2 c	Miso, mild yellow
2 Tbl	Red miso
1/2 c	Firm tofu
2 Tbl	Scallions, minced
	Lemon slivers

1) Prepare dashi according to recipe below.
2) Chop onion.
3) Mix both miso in water till a paste forms.
4) Add miso to broth, stir, add onions and tofu—heat till onion is tender.

Serve with garnish.

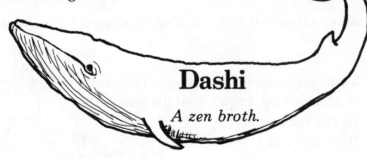

Dashi

A zen broth.

1 qt.	Water
1 piece	Kombu
2 tsp	Tamari
	Chopped scallions and cilantro as garnish

1) Rinse kombu and wipe dry.
2) Put into water and heat till almost boiling for 15 minutes.
3) Add tamari to taste. Serve with garnish or tiny cubed tofu.

Purifying Purees

Spinach Puree

1 lb	Spinach (frozen ok)
1	Onion
1	Garlic clove
2 Tbl	Lemon juice
2 c	Water or broth
1 Tbl	Aminos
2 Tbl	Nutritional yeast
1/2 tsp	Dill delight

1) Cook first three items in 1/2c water till tender, 10-15 minutes.
2) Put in blender or processor and puree one batch at a time.
3) Return to pot—add water, stir well, then add spices and heat until warm. Serve and garnish with a lemon twist.

Pea Puree

1 lb	Peas (frozen is easy)
1	Onion
1	Garlic clove
2 c	Water
1 Tbl	Liquid aminos
1 Tbl	Lemon juice
	Dash of nutmeg

1) Follow above directions.

Tropical Carrot Puree

4 lg	Carrots
1 lg	Onion
2 c	Water
1	Banana
1	Garlic clove
1 Tbl	Peanut butter (not so purifying, but delicious)
	Dash of aminos

1) Steam carrots and onion in water, puree in blender or processor, adding rest of ingredients.
2) Gently heat before serving.

Banana Saffron Carrot Puree

A delicately spiced puree with Indonesian flavors—terrific and good for you.

1/4 c	White wine or sake
2 c	Water
1 1/2 lbs	Fresh or frozen young carrots, chopped
1/2	Banana (approx. 4")
1	Garlic clove
1 tsp	Ginger, fresh, chopped
1 Tbl	Aminos
1/8 tsp	Fennel seeds, crushed
1/8 tsp	Chile flakes, crushed
Sm. pinch	Saffron threads, clove powder and wasabi powder
1/2 tsp	Curry powder
	Garnish with cilantro leaves

1) Bring liquids to a boil, add carrots and banana, cover and simmer for 10 minutes.
2) Puree, reserving a few carrots in pot. Add spices and puree several seconds.
3) Add reserved carrots, pulse chop briefly to keep a texture to puree.
4) Transfer back to pot and heat gently to meld flavors before serving.

Serves 3-4

Spicy Cilantro Zucchini

A creamy green soup spiced with red chile pulp.

4-5 c	Zucchini
1	Onion
1	Bell pepper
1/2 bunch	Cilantro, fresh
2 c	Water
1	Red chili, dried (approx. 5" long)
1/2 tsp	Oregano
1	Garlic clove
1-2 Tbl	Aminos (to taste)

1) Chop vegetables, add to pot of boiling water, cook until tender, covered on low. Puree, transfer back to pot.
2) Meanwhile cook chile in a small pan of boiling water for 10 minutes until soft. Squeeze pulp into puree.
3) Stir all together, adjust spices and serve hot.

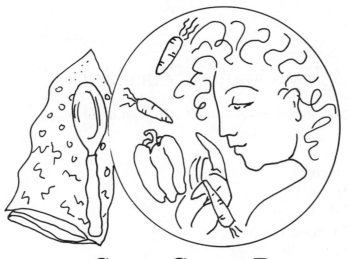

Corny Carrot Pepper

A delicious full bodied soup using fresh basil, cumin and sage.

1/2	Red bell pepper
1/2	Yellow bell pepper
5	Carrots
2	Onions
2 c	Corn, cut (frozen is OK)
1/2 bunch	Basil leaves, torn (approx. 1/2 c)
1	Garlic clove
2 Tbl	Bronner's liquid bouillon
1/2 tsp	Cumin and onion powder
2 Tbl	Brewers yeast
Pinch	Sage
	Cracked black pepper or cayenne to taste

1) Chop all veggies (first 6 items) and put into a large soup pot with about 2 c water, bring to boil, then cover and simmer for 15 minutes.
2) Transfer veggies to a blender or food processor and puree.
3) Return puree back to pot, stir in rest of ingredients, simmer until hot, add water if necessary and adjust seasoning to your taste.

Mediterranean Puree

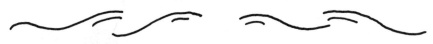

2 sm	Eggplants, peeled, chopped
1	Bunch Spinach leaves
1	Onion, chopped
4	Garlic cloves
1 c	Water or broth
2 Tbl	Lemon juice
3 Tbl	Liquid aminos
1 tsp	Oregano, basil mix or italian seasoning
1/2 Tbl	Honey
3 Tbl	Nutritional yeast
2 c	Broth or water (as needed)

1) Steam the first 5 ingredients for 20 minutes.
2) Puree in batches in a food processor till smooth, then return to pot.
3) Heat and add the rest. Cook for 20 minutes.

Puree of Simmered Greens

A delicate and mineral rich puree.

30-40	Beet leaves (fresh tender)
15-20	Swiss green chard leaves
2 1/2 c	Water or broth
2	Garlic cloves
2 tsp	Tamari
1/4 tsp	Ginger, grated and fresh

Cut 1/2 c carrot "flowers" to float in soup (See page 62)

1) Rinse and tear leaves into large pieces, put into a pot with water and bring to a boil, simmer until tender, 5-10 minutes (leaves will steam down dramatically in size).
2) Put greens in food processor or blender and puree. Put back in cooking pan (into broth that is there), add rest of ingredients, heat gently, serve.

Tomato Kale Soup

This is a hearty and delicious soup.

1 qt	Water
1 bunch	Kale
1/4	Red cabbage
1	Potato
1 lg	Carrot
5	Garlic cloves
28 oz can	Tomatoes, crushed
1/2 tsp	Coriander
1 tsp	Dill or dill delight (*see condiments)
1 Tbl	Onion powder

1) Chop kale, cabbage, carrot, cube the potato, press the garlic.
2) Put veggies into pot with water, bring to near boil, simmer covered 20 min. or so.
3) Add spices, simmer a couple more minutes.

Beet Borscht

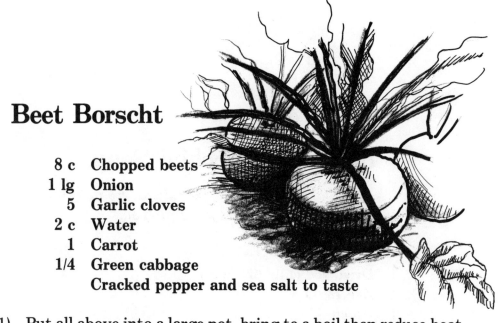

8 c	Chopped beets
1 lg	Onion
5	Garlic cloves
2 c	Water
1	Carrot
1/4	Green cabbage
	Cracked pepper and sea salt to taste

1) Put all above into a large pot, bring to a boil then reduce heat to simmer, covered, 15-20 minutes till beets are tender.
2) Transfer to a food processor or blender and puree, sections at a time. Returning each pureed batch to pot.
3) Serve hot or chilled and top with **Silken Sour Cream-less**—*see recipe p. 150*

Curried Carrot Puree

7 med	Carrots, chopped
2 c	Water
3	Garlic cloves, pressed
1 tsp	Fresh grated ginger
1/4 tsp	Cinnamon
1 tsp	Master curry
3 Tbl	Aminos or bouillon
1 Tbl	Maple syrup or apple concentrate
2 Tbl	Nutritional yeast

1) Steam carrots in water for 20 minutes or until tender.
2) Puree in food processor or blender, adding water from steaming, usually 2 batches will do.
3) Add garlic and ginger to last puree batch.
4) Put back in pot, add water for desired consistency and rest of spices. Heat gently till warm.

Red Chile Zucchini Soup

A rich deep color pervades this chile lovers delight.
Easy to make and good for you.

1	**Dried red chile (6" long)**
6	**Zucchinis**
1	**Onion**
2	**Garlic cloves**
1 c	**Water**
	Seasalt, cumin, oregano to taste
1 tsp	**Bouillon**

1) Lightly toast chile in oven—2 mins.
2) Stem and seed chile, tear in half and put it in a large pot with chopped zucchinis, onion and water, bring to a boil, then simmer 15 min. Scrape flesh from chile skin, discard skin.
3) Puree half the soup, return back to pan and stir in rest of seasoning. Serve warm.

Delicious served with **Chile corn bread** *and* **3-pepper black bean Salad.**

Native Chile Corn Chowder

A quick and easy healthy stew that is a favorite; the chile thickens and provides a rich background flavor.

5	Crook neck yellow squash
1	Bell pepper
1	Carrot
1/2 c	Parsley, packed
1 lg	Dried red chile (6″ long)
1 c	Corn, cut
2	Garlic cloves
1/2 tsp	Cumin
	Pinch of cinnamon
1 tsp	Aminos
	Water

1) Lightly toast chile only 2 minutes, seed and stem.
2) Chop veggies, put in a pot, add chile and 2 cups water and cover, bring to boil and then turn down to simmer for 10 minutes. Remove chile, scrape chile flesh into pot—discard skin.
3) Puree in food processor all but a few chunks of squash for texture.
4) Add corn, garlic and spices, add water to thin to desired consistency.

Leek Flower Soup

A thick creamy-like soup that melts in your mouth. Cauliflower and leek are heightened by the garlic and dill, simply divine.

1 lg	Head of cauliflower
1 lg	Leek
5	Garlic cloves
1 c	Beet (or other) greens
4 c	Water
2 Tbl	Aminos
1 Tbl	Nutritional yeast

To taste: Dill weed
Onion powder
Dash of cayenne

1) Cut up vegetables, boil water in a large soup pot, add veggies cook covered for 10 minutes on low.
2) Add garlic and spices, continue cooking 5 more minutes, until tender.
3) Puree 1/2 of soup (all greens) add back to pot—stir and serve.

Cream Soups—your creation:

Any vegetable can become "creamed" by steaming it, putting it into the blender or food processor with a bit of soft tofu and or soy milk, water from steaming and your favorite herbs and spices. This is a non fat version of the calorie—cholesterol ladden others, and is terrific! Happy discoveries.

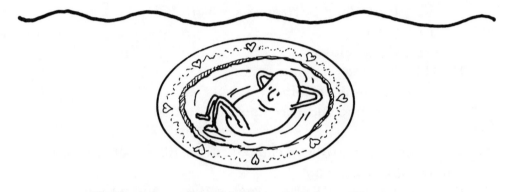

Cream of Sweet Lima Bean

2 c	Lima beans (frozen is easy)
1	Onion, chopped
1/2 c	Soy milk (vanilla soy milk adds a nice natural sweetness)
1/2	Fresh serrano chile (the small hot ones)
1 tsp	Aminos
2	Parsley sprigs
1	Marjoram sprig, fresh or oregano (leaves only)
	Water as needed, approx. 1 c

1) Steam or cook limas with onion till tender in water.
2) Put into a blender with rest of ingredients, adding water as needed (including steam water)
3) Serve, or heat gently in pan to keep warm.

Butternut Creme Soup

A wonderful way to have your squash.

1/2	1-foot long butternut squash
1 c	Water
1	Garlic clove
1/2 Tbl	Aminos
	Soy milk to thin
	Cayenne and curry powder to taste

1) Seed squash, cut into large chunks. Steam till tender in 1 c water, remove skin when cool.
2) Put into blender with steam water, blend, adding spices and soymilk to taste.
3) Heat to warm, serve.

For a really beautiful presentation, serve it in a pumpkin shell:

1) Cut top off pumpkin and hollow it out.
2) Pour boiling water inside—let sit 1 hr.
3) Pour out water.
4) Fill as is with soup.

Cream of Mushroom

1 1/2 lbs	Mushrooms, fresh
1	Onion, chopped
5	Garlic cloves
1 c	Celery and leaves
1/2 c ea	Water and wine
10.5 oz pk	Silken tofu
1 c	Soy milk
1 Tbl	Onion powder
1/4 c	Liquid aminos

1) Clean mushrooms with a wet towel, trim and chop coarsely with other vegetables.
2) Put veggies in water/wine mix and cook for 15 min. leaving to simmer on low.
3) Puree with tofu, soy milk and spices.
4) Return to pot and gently heat before serving.

Garnish with minced parsley.

Cream of Gold

A puree of curried golden zucchini and apple.

2 lg	Zucchinis (gold ones)—10-12" long each, 3" diameter
3/4 c	Broth or soy milk
2 tsp	Good fresh curry
1 1/2 Tbl	Honey or apple juice concentrate
1/4-1/2 tsp	Cinnamon
1 Tbl	Aminos, mineral bouillon or tamari

1) Cut up and steam zucchinis and apple in 1 cup water, approx. 10 minutes.
2) Puree when done, put back in pot and add rest of ingredients.

Spicy Eggplant Creme

2	Eggplants
2	Onions
2	Garlic cloves
1/2	Lemon juiced
1 c	Water or broth
2 c	Soy milk
2 tsp	Tamari (or 1 Tbl aminos)
1/2 tsp	Curry powder
1/4 tsp	(ea.) Cumin, and oregano
	Cracked black pepper and cayenne to taste
	Parsley as garnish

1) Slice eggplants lengthwise, sprinkle sea salt on top, let sweat 10-15 minutes, then blot dry.

2) Bake eggplants and onions in oven 30 minutes, then skin (or steam them both 15 minutes or until tender).

3) Puree them in food processor or blender adding everything but the soy milk.

4) Transfer to a soup pot and add soy milk, heat gently. Simmer 5 minutes or until thoroughly warm.

*Serve with crusty bread or whole grain crackers
and a crisp tossed salad.*

Thanksgiving Yam

A perfect cream soup for the Holidays, very easy to prepare. Try substituting sweet potatoes for a less sweet soup.

1 lg	Yam (approx. 2 c cooked)
1	Garlic clove
1 c	Apple cider, naturally spiced
1/3 c	Vanilla soymilk (or regular for a less sweet taste)
1/2 c	Water or more to thin
1/4 tsp	Curry powder (or to taste)

1) Chop and cook or steam yam in a little water till tender. Let cool, then skin.
2) Put everything into a blender and blend until thick, smooth and creamy. Adjust liquids to suit your personal taste. (More soy milk will yield a creamier texture).
3) Heat gently before serving.

Garnish with a small flower or leaf—fresh mint or cilantro will do nicely.

Sopa de Ajo

A Spanish garlic soup that works magic on colds.

1/2 c	Garlic, chopped (1 big bulb)
1 1/2 qts	Water
1/4 c	Rice
6'' piece	Kombu
1/8 tsp	Cayenne to taste
1 tsp	Olive oil
1 slice	Whole meal bread, toasted
1 Tbl	Aminos to taste

1) Prepare stock by rinsing Kombu and wiping dry.
2) Bring water to boil. Add Kombu and rice, reduce heat and simmer 15-20 minutes, remove Kombu.
3) Heat olive oil and aminos in skillet, add garlics, sauté lightly, add bread sliced into cubes. After a couple of minutes transfer 1/2 c broth into mixture then transfer it all back into stock pot.

Rosey Vegetable

A hearty vegetable soup with a gorgeous ruby color.

2 1/2 qts	Stock or water
1/2 c	Barley
3	Red potatoes
2 c	Celery, minced
2	Beets, chopped
1 c	Packed greens, chopped
1	Red onion, sliced
1/2 tsp	Red chile flakes, dried
1 Tbl ea	Lemon juice, coriander and tamari
1/2 Tbl	Sweet basil
1 tsp ea	Dill, cumin and onion powder
1/4 c	Aminos
2	Garlic cloves

1) Bring stock to a boil, add washed Barley, cover and simmer 15 minutes.
2) Add veggies to pot along with spices—simmer an hour or so.

Asian Carrot Soup

A delicate soup that melts in your mouth with a first impression of wow!

	Olive oil (no more than 1 Tbl)
2 Tbl	**Sake**
1/2	**Onion, chopped**
4 lg	**Garlic cloves, pressed**
4-5 lg	**Carrots**
3	**Zucchinis**
2 Tbl	**Miso**
2 Tbl	**Peanut butter**

1) Sauté the onion on medium high heat in a bit of olive oil and sake, add garlic after a few minutes. Stir well, reduce heat to simmer.

2) In a food processor—shred the rest of the vegetables—mix carrots in pot, stir well, then put zucchinis on top. Add water to just cover and put lid on pot. Simmer for 10 minutes.

3) Add miso and peanut butter (stir together first in a little water)

4) Add more water to cover ingredients, stir well, then cover to simmer 15 more min or until veggies are just tender.

Serve with a tofu marinade and a fresh green salad for a great color feast.

Southwest Bean Chowder

Chile, wine, lemons and cilantro give punch to this hearty veggie stew.

1 1/2 c	Dried garbanzos
1	Onion, sliced
4	Garlic cloves
2	Bay leaves
3	Carrots, finely chopped
1/4 c	Parsley, finely chopped
1 Tbl	Oregano
1/2 c	White wine, dry
1/2	Lemon juiced with slice of peel
16 oz	Tomatoes, crushed
2 med	Zucchinis, sliced in rounds
1 lg ear	Corn, shredded
1/2 tsp	Vegetable salt
1 Tbl	Cumin
1 tsp	Chile powder
1/4 c	Soy cheese of choice, shredded
	Cilantro for garnish

1) Rinse garbanzos and soak overnight in a pot of water. Bring to boil next morning, turn down to simmer.
2) Add the next 5 ingredients after 15 minutes. Cook 1/2 hr. covered on low.
3) Add the rest and cover for 20 more minutes.

Summer Minestrone

A satisfying minestrone with a nice flavor.

1 c	Garbanzos, white beans or red beans (soak overnight in 4 c water in a big enamel soup pot)
5 c	Shredded greens (beet, escarole or chard)
1 c	Zucchinis, fresh
1/4 c	Garlic, chopped
1 28oz	Can tomatoes with juice
1	Lemon slice
1 Tbl	Olive oil
bunch	Basil leaves (at least 1/2 c packed)
1/2 tsp ea	Pulverized fennel seeds and red chile flakes
1/2 Tbl	Italian herbs
1/4 c	Wine, dry

1) Bring water and beans to boil—reduce, add oil and simmer 1 hr.
2) Add rest of ingredients and more water to cover, put lid on, simmer 1 more hour, then turn off.

Very good with fresh grated soy parmesan cheese on each serving.

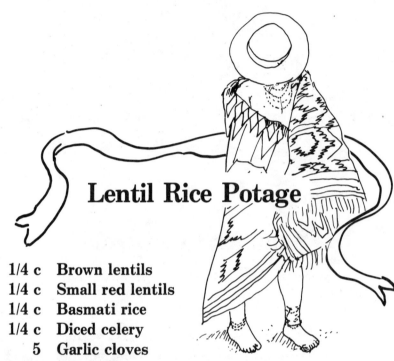

Lentil Rice Potage

1/4 c	Brown lentils
1/4 c	Small red lentils
1/4 c	Basmati rice
1/4 c	Diced celery
5	Garlic cloves
3 c	Shredded greens of your choice—kale, chard, endive
1	Onion, chopped
1 Tbl	Onion powder
3 Tbl	Tamari
1/2 Tbl ea	Coriander and cumin powder
1 Tbl	Italian herb blend
1 tsp	Crushed red peppers, dried

1) Put lentils and grains into large soup pot filled with boiling water, then add diced celery and garlic.
2) Cook for 15-20 minutes covered on low.
3) Add greens and rest of ingredients, simmer on low for 1 hour.

Top with gomasio

Tomato Barley Vegetable

A fragrant satisfying soup with many herbs.

1/2 gallon	Water
2 tsp	Fennel seeds
1 tsp	Cumin seeds
1 tsp	Thyme
1/4 tsp	Dried chile flakes
1/2 c	Barley
2 med.	Onions
3 c	Zucchini
28 oz (can)	Tomatoes, crushed
2 c	Cauliflower
1/2 c	Red wine
1 Tbl	Aminos or Bronner's
	Several fresh cilantro leaves and/or oregano leaves

1) Boil water in a large soup pot.
2) Grind spices in a blender, set aside.
3) Chop vegetables.
4) Add rinsed barley to soup pot. Then add veggies and spices. Simmer covered 15-25 minutes. Add wine last.

Serve 6. Garnish with herbs.

Green Chile Tortilla Soup

In the mood for a fiesta? Try this soup.

2 lg	Zucchinis, chopped coarsely
1	Anaheim green chile, chopped coarsely
1/2 can	Green chiles, roasted, and diced (1/2 lb.)
2 Tbl	Garlic, minced
1/2 c	Cilantro, minced
4	Corn tortillas (or leftover tortilla chips) cut in squares and toasted in oven briefly
1/4 c	Loose pack fresh oregano leaves (or 2 Tbl dried)
1 Tbl	Vegetable broth seasoning

1) Put all in large pot—cover with good water, bring to a boil and simmer till done (vegetables just soft) approx. 25 min.

2) Add sea salt or salt substitute to taste.

Ragin' Cajun Peanut Barley Stew

A spirited hearty soup.

3/4 c	Barley
1 qt.	Water (or veggie stock)
1 c	Celery, diced
2	Carrots, diced
2	Garlic cloves
1/4	Red cabbage, chopped
2 Tbl	Peanut butter
1/2 c	Peanuts, dry roasted and unsalted
2 Tbl	Dr. Bronner's mineral bouillon
1/4 c	Liquid aminos
128-oz can	Tomatoes, crushed
1 Tbl	Cajun spice (or to taste)
1/2 tsp	Dill salt

1) Bring water to a boil—add barley and half the celery, cover, simmer, 1 hour.
2) Add rest of veggies and spices and simmer another 1/2 hour.

Petite Orange Lentil Soup

A very fragrant aromatic soup with a luscious color.

1 1/2 qts.	Purified water
1 c	Petit orange lentils (masoor dal)
3 lg	Garlic cloves
1	Onion, chopped
1 sq. in.	Ginger, minced
1 tsp ea	Tumeric, coriander and tamari
1/2 tsp	Red chile flakes, crushed
16 oz can	Tomato paste
1/2	Orange peel gratings
	Dash nutmeg

1) Put lentils in pot with water, bring to boil and simmer, stirring occasionally.
2) Add next 6 ingredients. Skim foam off top, cook till tender 1/2 hr. or so.
3) Adjust seasonings and add orange peel and nutmeg.

Serve with Basmati rice and a crisp of salad, serves 4.

Dolphin Paradise

A Pacific sea vegetable-noodle soup featuring tofu & soba in a sesame miso broth.

1 oz	Sea vegetables*, dried
6-10 oz.	Soba noodles
4 qts.	Pure water
1	Onion, chopped
1	Carrot, minced
1	Zucchini, chopped
6 oz.	Firm tofu (fried 5-spice), cubed
2 Tbl	Miso, mild golden mixed into a paste with water
1 tsp	Fresh ginger, pressed thru garlic press
1 tsp	Chili-sesame oil
	Toasted sesame seeds for garnish

1) Bring water to boil in a soup pot, cook sea vegetables for 10 min.
2) Meanwhile, pulse chop veggies in food processor.
3) Add soba noodles and onion to pot, cook till al dente, pull out and drain separately.
4) Add rest of vegetables to broth, cook 10 minutes, then add noodles and spices simmer a few moments before serving.

Found in natural food stores.

Tofu Cioppino

2 qts	Stock from veggies (onions, garlic, celery tops, bay leaves and peppercorns)
1 pk	Tofu, firm, marinated in:
	1/2 lemon juice, 3 garlic cloves, pressed, 1/8 tsp saffron threads, 1 Tbl aminos, sprig of basil
32 oz. can	Tomatoes, crushed
2	Onions, minced
1 c	Potatoes, small cubed
1 lg	Garlic clove
1/4 c	Red wine
Pinch	Cayenne, cardamon powder and saffron to taste

Garnish with grated soy parmesan cheese, or drizzled good olive oil.

1) Prepare the tofu a day ahead for the most flavor: Press all water out of firm tofu (lay a towel over it and place a heavy pot on top), cube then marinate it 4 hrs. or more.
2) Simmer stock 2 hours, then strain.
3) Add next five items, simmer 1 hour or until potatoes are cooked.
4) Adjust seasonings.

Serve with crusty bread and crisp salad.

Note: you can cut the tofu in slender sticks 1'' long, cube them or mash them and put into cheese cloth and twist into ball for variations.

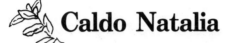 # Caldo Natalia

A fragrant Mexican vegetable soup—my favorite—served over rice and topped with more delicacies.

5	Anaheim chiles (long green ones)
5	Zucchinis
2 lg	Carrots
1 c	Red onion
15 oz can	Garbanzos
1/2 tsp	Ground cloves
8	Garlic cloves
1 Tbl ea	Oregano and cumin
2 Tbl	Aminos
1 tsp	Cracked black pepper
A few	Fresh basil sprigs
2 qrts	Stock or water

1) Slice chiles lengthwise, remove seeds and chop, slice zucchinis and carrots, chop onion.

2) Heat up stock or water, add vegetables, pressed garlic and spices heat to boiling. Then quickly reduce to simmer, cover and cook till tender approx. 15 minutes.

3) Serve with **Natalia's Rice** (see recipe in grain section) and serve with separate bowls of:

> **Chopped tomatoes**
> **Cilantro**
> **Sliced avocados**
> **Minced onion**

Cilantro Barley Stew

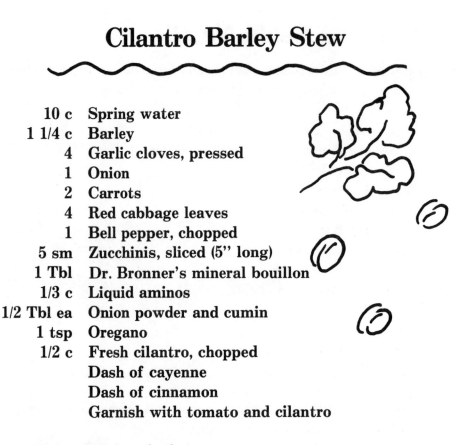

10 c	Spring water
1 1/4 c	Barley
4	Garlic cloves, pressed
1	Onion
2	Carrots
4	Red cabbage leaves
1	Bell pepper, chopped
5 sm	Zucchinis, sliced (5" long)
1 Tbl	Dr. Bronner's mineral bouillon
1/3 c	Liquid aminos
1/2 Tbl ea	Onion powder and cumin
1 tsp	Oregano
1/2 c	Fresh cilantro, chopped
	Dash of cayenne
	Dash of cinnamon
	Garnish with tomato and cilantro

1) Bring water to a boil.
2) Add barley and garlic to water. Bring to boil, turn down to simmer, cover, cook 1/2 hr.
3) Finely chop the onions, carrots and cabbage, slice the zucchini. Add vegetables, simmer for 1/2 hour more.
4) Add spices and simmer a few more minutes till all has blossomed.

Top each bowl with 1/4 tomato, seeded and chopped, and a few cilantro leaves.

Couscous Stew

The spices are many, but create a tapestry of wonderful seasoning, fragrance and color.

7-8	**Potatoes**
6	**Carrots**
2	**Onions**
1/2 bunch	**Parsley**
4 1/2 qts	**Kombu broth (see recipe)**
5 lg	**Garlic cloves**
1 c	**Radishes**
5	**Cherry tomatoes**
1/4 c	**Couscous**
1/4 c	**Tomato paste**
1 Tbl ea	**Onion powder, coriander, basil, dill, cooking sherry and tamari**
1 tsp ea	**Cumin, chili powder, tumeric**
	Ginger, freshly grated (put through garlic press)
1/2 tsp ea	**Nutmeg and cardamon**
	Dash cayenne
2 tsp	**Arrowroot powder mixed with 1/4 c water**

1) Dice and peel potatoes, chop carrots, onions and parsley, quarter radishes put into large pot of Kombu broth.
2) Bring to boil, then turn to low, simmer covered for 20 minutes.
3) Stir in rest of ingredients.
4) Heat till warmed throughout (approx. 15 minutes). Make sure couscous is tender before serving.

Smoky Lentil Soup

Hearty tofu pup'n lentil stew.

1 Tbl	Aminos
1 c	Washed lentils
1 lg	Leek, sliced
1 lg	Carrot, minced
3 lg	Garlic cloves
32 oz can	Tomatoes, cut
2	Tofu browners or pups chopped
1 Tbl	Cumin seeds crushed or powder
3 sprigs	Fresh basil tops
1/2 tsp	Chile powder

1) Sauté 1 Tbl aminos with leek, carrot, garlic in pot—add browners and lentils, stir a few minites.
2) Add 1 can peeled stewed tomatoes and their juice, cover with water, bring to boil, add spices.
3) Simmer 2 hours—or turn the heat off and keep it covered all day. Reheat before serving.

Hearty Vegetable

A meal in itself, begin this in the morning and let it sit covered without a flame until the evening.

1 lg	Pot of pure water (approx. 3 qrts)
1/2 c	Aduki beans
1/2 c	Barley
1/2	Eggplant
2	Carrots
5	Garlic cloves
	Few clusters of parsley
	Few chives
1/2 c	Peas, fresh or frozen
1 tsp ea	Tumeric, curry and cumin
1 Tbl ea	Coriander, ground, onion and basil (dried)
2 tsp	Dill or dill delight
1/4 tsp	Red chili flakes
2	Zucchinis
1 c	Fresh seeded tomatoes
2 Tbl	Dr. Bronner's mineral bouillon

1) Bring pot of water to boil, add beans and barley continue cooking 10-15 minutes.
2) Shred next 5 ingredients in food processor or chop fine.
3) Add to pot along with spices and peas. Continue cooking 1/2 hour covered on low then turn off and let everything melt into a harmonious glee.
4) When you return near dinner time add sliced zucchinis, chopped tomatoes and seasoning. Simmer 10 minutes and serve.

Chilled Papaya Bisque

A soothing tropical puree with a hint of lime and mint. A nice prelude to spicey meals.

3 c	Papaya flesh, chopped
1/2 c	Coconut milk
5 Tbl	Chopped dates or date pieces
1/4 c	Lime juice, fresh
1 c	Pure water
1/4 c	Orange juice
7	Mint leaves

1) Blend until smooth and creamy, chill before serving, garnish each bowl with a mint leaf.

Chilled Cucumber Soup

A light mint colored icy refresher

3 lg	Cucumbers
6 oz	Tofu
1/2 tsp	Onion powder
6-9	Fresh mint or basil leaves
1 tsp	Veg. salt substitute
1	Lemon, juiced
3/4 c	Peppermint tea, brewed
	(Adding soy milk or soy yogurt will create a creamy consistency)
	Cracked pepper to taste

1) Peel and chop cucumbers—seed them too.
2) Process or blend them in batches, adding rest of items.

Chill before serving. Float a small pink flower or nasturtium on top for color contrast.

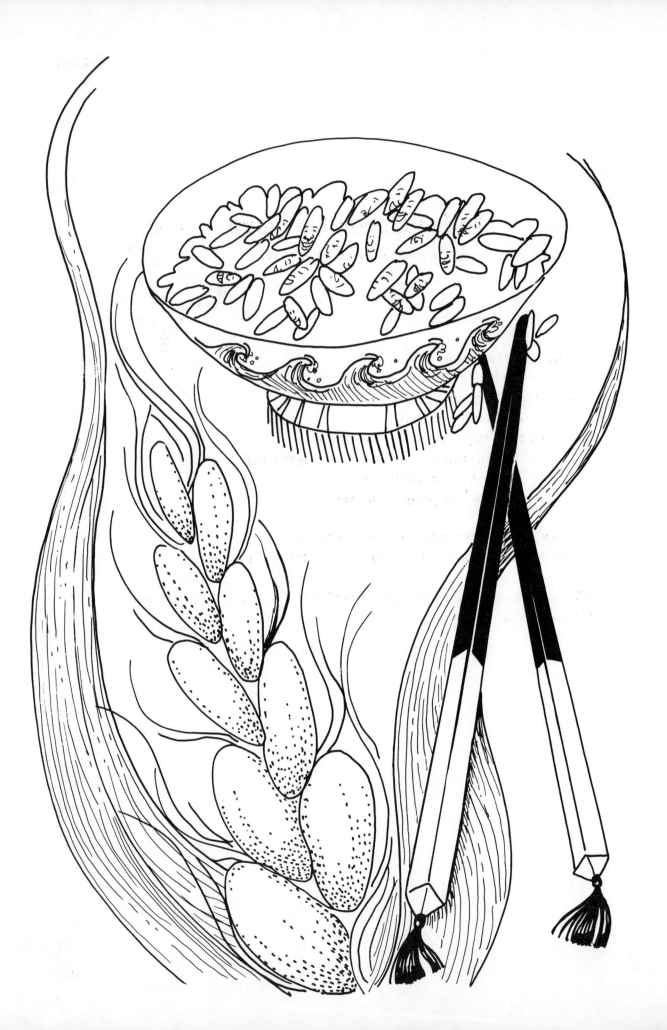

GRAINS, BEANS & BREAD

GRAINS

Ah yes, those delectable carbohydrates few can live without. Grains truly are a staple in vegetarian cooking, and have been a mainstay in all people's diets throughout our global history.

The cultivation of grains represents our working with mother Earth. Since antiquity they have been found entombed in pyramids and burial chambers.

Whole grains provide valuable nutrition and roughage not obtainable from refined flour products. It is therefore important to consume these "kernals of life" whole, whether sprouted, steamed, sauteed or baked. They are delicious in salads, soups, breads and casseroles or simply by themselves, as in the following recipes.

Indian Millet

1 c	Millet, rinsed thru a colander
1 Tbl	Curry powder
1 Tbl	Black mustard seeds
1 sm	Red onion, sliced
1 1/2 c	Boiling water
1 Tbl	Aminos
1 c	Coconut milk
2	Tomatoes, chopped, seeded

1) Sauté first 3 things on medium heat in skillet till golden, approx. 3 minutes.
2) Add onion, continue stirring.
3) Add water, aminos and coconut milk, stir and cover, simmer 20 minutes.
4) Fork in tomatoes.

Garden Couscous

3/4 c   **Couscous**
1 c   **Water**
      Dash of sea salt
1/2   **Onion**
1   **Carrot**
1/2 c   **Peas**
1   **Garlic clove, pressed**
1 Tbl   **Aminos**
1/4 c   **Fresh herbs, chopped (thyme, basil, mint, parsley,
       watercress, whatever you wish)**
2 Tbl   **Wine**
      Cracked pepper

1) Heat water to boil, add couscous and sea salt. Stir to boil, cover for 5 minutes on low heat, turn off.
2) Chop veggies finely, put in skillet with herbs, aminos and wine. Sauté—add water if necessary, cover and simmer till tender.
3) Fluff couscous with a fork into vegetable mix, stir to combine. Serve hot.

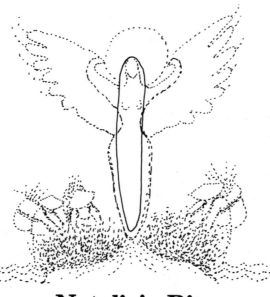

Natalia's Rice

Unamimously voted the best rice

3/4 c	Basmati, jasmine or long grain rice
1/2	Lemon, juiced
1 Tbl	Vegetable oil
1/4 c	White wine
1/4 c	Salsa fresca (can substitute 1 garlic clove, pressed; 1 tsp cumin; 1 Tbl onion, minced; 1 tomato, seeded and chopped)
1 c	Hot water
1 Tbl	Aminos

1) Rinse rice and cover with hot water for 10 minutes, drain.
2) Pour lemon juice over it, toss.
3) Heat oil in skillet, add rice, stir till golden, add wine, salsa, water and seasoning, stir well, cover and cook for 12-15 minutes.

Yellow Rice

2 c	Long grain brown rice
4 c	Boiling water
1 1/2 tsp	Turmeric
1/2 Tbl	Soya lecithin spread
	Cracked pepper and 1 Tbl aminos

1) Bring water to a boil, add rinsed rice and seasoning.
2) Cover and simmer for 30 minutes, then turn off heat and keep lid on another 5-10 minutes.

Wild Rice

3 c	Water
1 c	Wild rice
1/4 c	Red wine
1 sm	Red onion
1/2 tsp	Vegetable salt

1) Bring water to boil.
2) Dice onion, rinse rice.
3) Add everything to boiling water, cover and simmer for 1 hour.

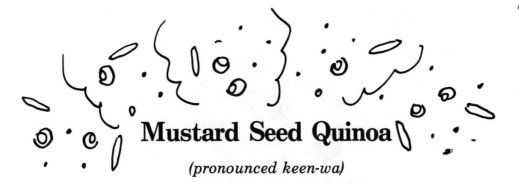

Mustard Seed Quinoa

(pronounced keen-wa)

An ancient supergrain and complete protein, containing the highest amount of essential fatty acids of any other grain. It has a light, nutty taste. The addition of mustard seeds and Basmanti rice give it an Indian flair.

1 c	Quinoa
1 c	Rice—jasmine or basmati (white)
3 1/2 c	Water
1 Tbl	Black mustard seeds
1/2 Tbl	Aminos or 1/2 tsp sea salt
	Pinch of cayenne

1) Add seeds to small skillet (have lid ready to cover them once seeds begin to pop).
2) Bring water to boil, add rinsed grains, and rest of ingredients. Cover and cook on low 15 minutes.

Toasted Anise Rice

1 c	Basmati Rice
1/2 Tbl	Anise seeds
1 3/4 c	Water
1/2 tsp	Sea salt

1) Bring water to boil.
2) Toast anise seeds in toaster oven till light brown.
3) Add seeds, rice and salt to pot. Return to boil, then cover and simmer 15-20 minutes.

Quick Sushi Rice

Add this sauce to 2 cups of just cooked short grain brown rice.

1-1/2 Tbl	Rice vinegar
1 Tbl	Honey
1/2 Tbl	Soy sauce
	Dash of mirin

1) Heat up mixture in small saucepan, stir to dissolve.
2) Cool to room temperature, then cut into rice with a large wooden paddle-spoon.

Miso Sesame Rice

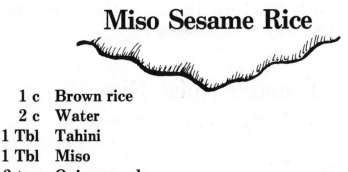

1 c	Brown rice
2 c	Water
1 Tbl	Tahini
1 Tbl	Miso
2 tsp	Onion powder
1/4 c	Warm water

1) Bring water to a boil, add rinsed rice, cover and simmer 35-40 minutes.
2) Mix rest of ingredients into a paste, then stir into rice when done.

Celebration Millet

2	Jalapeños, seeded
1	Lemon, juiced
1	Orange, juiced
1 c	Coconut, grated
1/2 c	Cilantro leaves
1/2 c	Mint leaves
3/4 c	Coconut milk
1	Garlic clove
1 3/4 c	Stock or water
1 1/2 c	Millet
2 Tbl	Pine nuts, lightly toasted
1 Tbl	Black mustard seeds
2 Tbl	Raisins (golden ones)

1) Put first 6 items in food processor and mince, stop and scrape down when necessary.
2) Strain out roughage, and put liquid in pot.
3) Add the coconut milk, pressed garlic and water to pot , bring to a boil.
4) Stir in well-washed millet and cover, simmer for 40-45 minutes.
5) Toss with last three items.

Serve with a crisp cucumber salad and **Tofu Thai Peanut Sauce** *or* **Coconut Peanut Sauce.**   *Serves 2-4.*

Vegetable Polenta Frittata

2 Tbl	Aminos
1 lg	Garlic clove
1	Onion
2	Zucchinis
1/3 c	Instant cereal (brown rice cream, oat bran, cream of wheat)
2 Tbl ea	Parsley, fresh, and soy parmesan cheese
1 tsp ea	Oregano, basil and nutritional yeast
1/2 c	Mushrooms
	Dash red chili flakes and curry
	Broth or water

1) Heat aminos in skillet, sauté sliced onions, cubed and skinned eggplant, quartered mushrooms, pressed garlic, and chopped zucchini.
2) Stir in cereal, slowly add broth or water stirring to a smooth consistency. Add herbs and spices and simmer 3-5 minutes.
3) Pour into a lightly oiled ring mold, baking dish or pie dish and refrigerate till firm.
4) Slice polenta and sauté in a little aminos or heat in oven. Serve sauce of choice on top, I like a simple marinara on the side.

If you like this dish, try changing the spices and vegetables for a different flavor.
For Mexican, try green chiles and tomatoes sauteed with cumin and chili powder, serve with **Meximato Sauce.**

Mushroom Kasha

A savory mushroom and toasted buckwheat pilaf

1 c	Kasha
1 1/2 c	Boiling water
1/2 lb	Mushrooms (2 c)
1	Garlic clove
1 sm	Onion
1 Tbl	Aminos
1/2	Lemon, juiced
1/4 c	Parsley, chopped
1/4 c	Red wine

1) Rinse kasha, put into a glass bowl, pour 1 c boiling water over it and let soak 15-30 minutes.

2) Slice mushrooms and onion, then sauté in large skillet in aminos, wine, garlic and lemon juice. Stir continually for a couple of minutes.

3) Add strained kasha and stir, add parsley.

4) Then add rest of water, cover for 15 minutes on low. Fluff with fork before serving.

Spiced Indian Dal

Dal is a staple food in Indian cooking—resembles small green split peas. Serve with a **Vegetable Curry***, **Mustard Seed (Quinoa) Rice*** *and* **Fig Chutney***.

1/2 c	**Dal**
3 3/4 c	**Water**
1 Tbl	**Onion seeds**
2 Tbl	**Aminos**
1 tsp	**Chopped fresh ginger**
1 lg	**Garlic clove**
1 tsp	**Coriander**
1/4 tsp	**Cardamon**
1	**recipe for mustard seed rice**

1) Wash dal (looks like small split peas).
2) Bring water to boil in medium pot.
3) Add dal and onion seeds. Bring to boil, cover and reduce to simmer for 30 min.
4) Press ginger thru garlic press, and add to pot along with rest of seasonings.
5) Puree dal in blender for a smoother sauce, transfer back into saucepan, heat before serving over rice.

*See recipes page 264, 205, 153, respectively.

Outrageous Pot o' Beans

*The aroma of homemade spicy beans can cure anything! This makes
a large pot, and leftovers can be frozen. Great in soups, with tortillas,
or pureed into a sauce.*

2 c	Your favorite dried beans (garbanzo, white black, red, soy)
2	Red California Chiles, dried (5" long)
1	Bell pepper, chopped
1	Onion, chopped
1 1/2 c	Tomato puree (or crushed tomatoes)
5	Garlic cloves, minced
1 Tbl	Cumin seeds
2 Tbl	Onion powder
1 tsp ea	Cumin powder, sweet basil, oregano, chile powder
	Dash of clove powder

1) Rinse beans and put in a large pot, cover with water and let sit overnight (10 hrs.).
2) Bring water in pot to boil, cover and simmer 2 hours.
3) Add chiles (breaking off stem, shake out seeds). Cook another 20 minutes.
4) Add rest of ingredients, return to a boil on high, then simmer 1 more hour till soft.
5) Scrape chile pulp back into pot, throw away skins—adjust seasonings or add water if needed.

Aduki Bean and Brown Rice Pot

Easy! Cook it all in one pot for a satisfying meal.

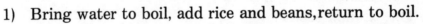

4 1/4 c	Water
1 c	Brown rice, rinsed
1 c	Aduki beans, rinsed
1	Red onion, chopped
1	Green bell pepper or anaheim chile
2	Garlic cloves, minced
1/4 tsp	Cayenne
2 tsp	Cumin
1 Tbl	Chile powder
1 tsp	Vegetable salt

1) Bring water to boil, add rice and beans, return to boil.
2) Add veggies and seasonings. Cover and simmer 45 min. to 1 hr.

Serve with tortillas and garnish of Salsa Fresca:

1/4 c	Cilantro, chopped
1 c	Tomatoes, chopped
1/2 c	Onion, chopped
1	Jalapeño chile, seeded and chopped
	(Avocado slices on the side if desired)

Mix in one bowl.

Féjoada

(Fay-jo-wah'-dah)
I substitute soy sausages in this Brazilian staple

Beans:

2 qts	Water
2 c	Black beans
1 tsp	Ginger, pressed

2 Tbl (ea)	Wine, lemon juice
1/2 lb	Soy sausage (spiced)
1 Tbl	Garlic, minced
3/4 c	Onions, sliced
2	Tomatoes, chopped
1	Jalapeño, roasted (see page 27)
1/2 tsp	Sea salt
1/4 tsp	Fresh ground black pepper
2 tsp	Grated orange rind
	Cayenne to taste

1) Bring water to boil, add rinsed beans and ginger, boil 2 min. then cover and let soak 1 hr. (or soak overnight).
2) Return to boil, then turn to low, simmer 2 hrs. covered, till tender. Chop vegetables.
3) Sauté liquids, garlic and onion in a big skillet, add soy sausages and cook for 5 minutes, add rest of ingredients.
4) Add beans with a slotted spoon into skillet, adding bean liquid to thin. Simmer 15 minutes or until thick, scraping bottom and turning often. Can be frozen.

Serve with tortillas or rice, salad, and a big platter of fruit with lime wedges for dessert.

Green Chile Corn Bread

A Southwest corn bread that is addicting.

1 c	Wholewheat pastry or unbleached flour
1 c	Whole grain corn meal
3 Tbl	Date, turbinado or brown sugar
5 tsp	Baking powder
1 1/2 tsp	Egg replacer with 2 Tbl water
1 c	Soy milk
2 Tbl	Oil
1 sm can	Green chiles, chopped
1/2 tsp ea	Sea salt, cumin and onion powder
1 ear	Corn shredded (approx. 1/2 c)

1) Stir wet ingredients together.
2) Sift dry into wet, stir in chiles and corn.
3) Oil a 9″ baking pan and bake at 375° for 35 minutes or until light brown.

Serve with **3 Pepper Black Bean Salad.**

Tempeh Herb Bread

*A spicy round wheat bread with crumbled tempeh and the aroma
of Italian sausage.*

1/4 c	Warm water
1 pk	Active dry yeast
3/4 c	Warm soy milk
1 Tbl	Honey
2 1/2 c	Wholewheat pastry flour
1/2 c	Unbleached flour
6 oz	Tempeh cutlet
1 Tbl	Olive oil
1 tsp ea	Soy sauce, basil, oregano, fennel seeds, red chili flakes*, onion and garlic powder.

1) Sprinkle yeast over warm water—let sit 5 min.
2) Heat soy sauce and 1/2 the oil, sauté crumbled tempeh on low,
    stirring for several minutes—set aside and stir in herbs.
3) Add soy milk and honey to yeast, add flour 1c at a time, knead
    in till smooth approx. 6-10 min. Let rise, covered for an hour
    in an oiled bowl.
4) Punch down, spread flat, work in tempeh and form into a ball.
    Press an inverted can on top for an interesting shape. Let rise
    30 min. on a baking sheet.
5) Brush with olive oil and bake 375° for 30 minutes (should sound
    hollow if tapped), slice in wedges.

VEGETABLE SIDE DISHES

Baking Vegetables Whole

Vegetables with skins on them bake the best. Wash veggies first, and pierce potatoes with a fork to allow steam to escape (it's not necessary to pierce yams or sweet potatoes). Unpeeled beets, garlic and onions can be baked whole. Slice bottoms off onions and sit them in a shallow baking pan of water so the dripping juices don't burn. Average temperature is 375° for baking.

Broiled Vegetables

For a change of pace try this quick method of using a hot 550° oven, use the top rack in your oven.

1) Slice veggies thin to ensure even cooking.
2) Brush soft veggies with tamari, aminos, or a garlic-herb-oil mixture so they don't dryout too fast.
3) Put veggies on cookie sheet, check every couple of minutes because they cook fast! If veggies brown quicker than they cook, move rack down one notch.

Try mushrooms (cap side down) with a drop of aminos inside caps, skewer veggies and place over a pan to catch juice, or try eggplant slices topped with tomato sauce, herbs and soy cheese.

Steamed Vegetables with Dill

Fresh dill weed and chives dress up quick steamed veggies for a great side dish.

1 lg	Broccoli stalk
1/2 head	Cauliflower
2	Red rose potatoes (approx. 1 1/2 cups)
2 Tbl	Dill, fresh, minced
1 Tbl	Chives, fresh, minced
1 Tbl	Lemon juice
1 Tbl	Aminos
2 Tbl	Water from steaming

1) Cut broccoli into spears, skin and quarter to stalk. Break cauliflower into florettes, cube potatoes.
2) Put steamer basket into a large pot of water, add water 1'' deep, add veggies and cover, bring to a boil, then simmer until al dente (not too soft) about 10-12 minutes.
3) Remove steamer basket full of veggies and set aside. Reserve steam water in another vessel.
4) Add herbs and 2 Tbl stock to pot, add veggies and toss altogether with rest of items.

Serve warm. Feeds 2-4.

Ginger Longbeans

Wonderful on **Cabbage Noodles.**

1/4 c	Water
1 bunch	Japanese long beans
12 med	Mushrooms
3	Celery ribs
1 Tbl	Ginger
1/4 c	Cooking sherry
1 Tbl	Tamari
1/2 tsp	Toasted sesame oil

1) Chop beans in 2″ lengths, slice vegetables, mince ginger.
2) Heat water in wok on high, add vegetables, cook for 8 minutes.
3) Stir in last three items, turn off heat and cover.

Simmering Lotus Root

Slightly sweet and crisp side dish

1 sm	Lotus root—2" diameter*
1 1/2 c	Water with some rice vinegar added

Sauce:

3 Tbl	Mirin
1 Tbl	Tamari
2 Tbl	Hot water
pinch	Umeboshi paste
1 Tbl	Brown sesame seeds as garnish
	Dash of toasted sesame oil

1) Peel fresh root, slice off ends, then slice thinly.
2) Put into saucepan with water and vinegar, bring to a boil, then simmer on low 10-15 minutes, drain.
3) Stir rest of ingredients together and pour over cooked roots in same small pan cooking briefly. Sprinkle seeds generously on top. (Top brown briefly for extra flavor).

Peeled, sliced, boiled lotus are found in oriental grocers, if used omit steps 1 & 2.

Sauteed Fennel Bulb

An aromatic delicacy.

3-4	Whole fennel bulbs sliced into "patties"
8 lg	Garlic cloves, unpeeled
2 Tbl	Olive oil
1/4 c	Water
2 Tbl	Fennel leaves, chopped, as garnish
	Sea salt or liquid aminos and pepper to taste

1) Put 1 Tbl water in skillet, bring to med high heat, add oil, put fennel slices face down, add garlics with jackets on so they don't burn.
2) Stir, shake, and flip fennel over when browned on each side.
3) Sprinkle with sea salt and pepper, pour water in and cover for 20 minutes until tender.
4) Garnish with fennel leaves.

New Zealand Spinach

1 Tbl	Water
2 tsp	Safflower or olive oil
1	Garlic clove, minced
1 lg bunch	Your favorite greens
	Sesame seeds, toasted as garnish

1) Heat water and oil in wok—add garlic—stir.
2) Then add cleaned greens—cover with 1/4 c water. Steam 5 minutes.
   Add soy sauce as seasoning if desired.

Turnip Gratin

Try with other roots, too!

1 Tbl	Liquid bouillon
6	Turnips
3/4	Tofu cream sauce, see page 134
1/4 c	Bread crumbs

1) Grate turnips, saute in skillet in liquid bouillon.
2) Put in baking dish, cover with creme sauce.
3) Top with 1/4 c bread crumbs and bake 30 minutes at 375°.

Chayote Squash and Corn

A Native American dish

2	**Chayotes**
2 ears	**Corn**
1	**Garlic, clove**
2 Tbl	**Red peppers or pimentos, roasted**
3 Tbl	**Water**
1 Tbl	**Liquid aminos**

1) Cut squash into chunks, shuck corn, press garlic, chop peppers and stir in a pot with rest of ingredients.

2) Bring to boil with lid on, then simmer on low 20 or so minutes until tender.

*Note—if chayotes are tough, you may prefer to cook them first for 10 minutes then add rest of ingredients.

Spaghetti Squash Americana

Makes 4 moderate servings—but it is so delicious, you may wish to double the recipe and freeze leftovers. Kids go for this, too.

1/2	**Spaghetti squash**
1/2 c	**Soy cheese, grated**
1 clove	**Garlic, pressed**
	Fresh cracked black pepper
	Nutmeg—freshly grated is best

1) Scoop seeds out of squash and steam in large pot with a bit of water for 45 min. until tender.
2) Scoop flesh out of squash and stir in bowl with rest of goodies, season to taste.

Serve steamed vegetables on top with fresh grated soy cheese and lemon juice. Zucchinis, mushrooms and bell peppers are nice.

Sauteed Escarole or Chard

A delicious way to eat your greens.

1 lg	Bunch of Escarole or Green chard
2 Tbl	Cooking sherry
1 Tbl ea	Lemon juice and aminos
2	Garlic cloves
2 Tbl	Grated soy parmesan cheese
	Water as needed

1) Slice greens, if using chard cut ribs out in a "V" shape, slice ribs.
2) Sauté greens in liquids in a heavy skillet. Stir frequently on low heat, 10 minutes.
3) Press garlic on top when almost done, toss in soy parmesan. Drizzle a bit of olive oil on top if desired. Serve warm.

Swedish Red Cabbage

Serves 4 as a side dish—great with hearty foods like broiled tempeh and potatoes, yields a sweet-sour taste—good chilled too.

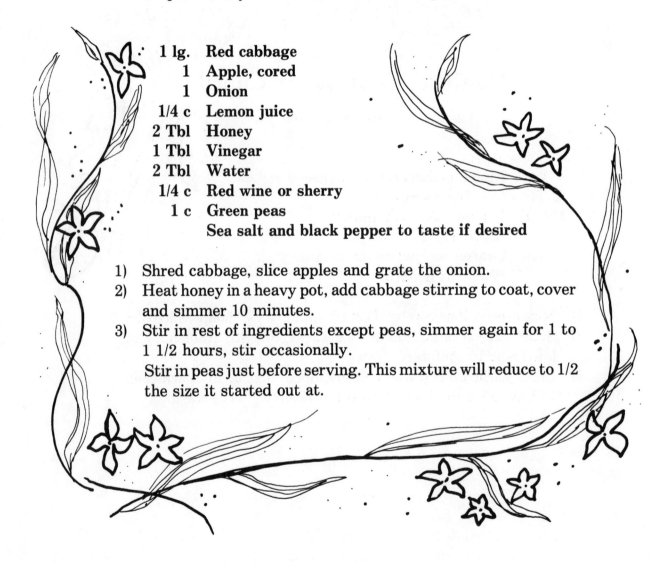

1 lg.	Red cabbage
1	Apple, cored
1	Onion
1/4 c	Lemon juice
2 Tbl	Honey
1 Tbl	Vinegar
2 Tbl	Water
1/4 c	Red wine or sherry
1 c	Green peas
	Sea salt and black pepper to taste if desired

1) Shred cabbage, slice apples and grate the onion.
2) Heat honey in a heavy pot, add cabbage stirring to coat, cover and simmer 10 minutes.
3) Stir in rest of ingredients except peas, simmer again for 1 to 1 1/2 hours, stir occasionally.

   Stir in peas just before serving. This mixture will reduce to 1/2 the size it started out at.

Sherried Shrooms

A magical side dish for two.

10 lg	Mushrooms, quartered
1/2 c	Cooking sherry
4	Garlic cloves, pressed
1 tsp ea	Onion powder and soy sauce
	Water as needed

1) Heat sherry in skillet, add garlic, stir, then add mushrooms and continue stirring on medium heat.
2) Add rest of ingredients, simmer approx. 10 minutes more.

Jamaican Eggplant

Succulent eggplants in a coconut spiced sauce.

2 sm	Eggplants
1	Red bell pepper, sliced
1 lg	Garlic clove, pressed
1″	Piece ginger, pressed
1/4 c	Coconut milk
1/4 c	Water
1/2	Lemon, juiced
	Sea salt, black pepper and cayenne to taste

1) Skin and halve eggplant, slice into 1/4″ thick semi-circles.
2) Heat lemon juice, water and coconut milk in wok.
3) Sauté all in hot wok till tender, 5-10 minutes.

Serves 3-4

Whipped Eggplant

*You can serve this chilled as a dip for pitas too, just stir in a bit
of plain soy yogurt or tofunaise.*

2 sm	Eggplants
1	Lemon, juiced
2	Garlic, cloves
1/2 tsp	Curry powder
2 Tbl	Tahini
2 tsp	Tamari
pinch	Cayenne and cracked pepper

1) Slice eggplants lengthwise, lightly salt and leave them to sweat
   it out for 15 minutes.
2) Blot off water and salt with a paper towel and bake 400° for
   30 minutes.
3) Skin when cool, chop flesh and put it all into a blender or food
   processor and puree till smooth.

Or serve as a soup—thin to consistency desired.

Potatoes, Peppers & Ale

A spicy and hearty side dish. The Ale will carmelize in heat and create a fantastic seasoning.

3 lg	Russet potatoes
1 lg	Onion
1	Anaheim pepper
2	Jalapeño peppers
1/4 c	Dark beer or ale
1 Tbl	Tamari or Bronner's
	Cracked pepper
1/2 c	Grated soy cheese, cheddar style

1) Peel and cube potatoes in 1/2″ sections.
2) De-seed peppers and slice along with onion.
3) Put in baking dish and toss with rest of ingredients, except soy cheese. Bake at 400° for 45 minutes. Stir in soy cheese when done.

Heavenly Glazed Apricot Yams

A sweet and spicy treat, perfect for holiday meals. Be sure to use fresh ginger root.

2	Sweet potatoes
2	Yams
1 c	Apricot halves, soaked
1/4 c	Lemon juice
1/4 c	Maple syrup or honey
1 Tbl	Ginger, freshly chopped
	Fresh grated nutmeg

1) Bake yams and potatoes until tender, approx. 35 min. at 350°.
2) Meanwhile, stir lemon, maple syrup and ginger together (press ginger through a garlic press to release its flavor).
3) Slice roots, arrange half the roots on a glass baking dish. Pour half the lemon mix on top, then arrange half the apricots on top, repeat process with second layer.
4) Bake until warmed in a 375° oven (approx. 15-20 min.).

Makes 6-10 servings

MAIN DISHES

MAIN DISHES

At last, an eclectic montage of vegetarian main dishes prepared without dairy products. These dishes provide a down home comfort, and yet aspire to new and unusual global gastronomical sensations.

My fascination with other cultures and foods has led to many adventurous experiments as you will see in the following recipes.

These multi-ethnic dishes include American nouvelle cooking, exotic south of the border creations, crowd pleasing Italian entrees, Thai delights, and other vegetarian favorites; all prepared with your ultimate health in mind.

These dishes will leave you feeling lighter than the foods you might be used to eating. I have many titillating tofu and tempeh recipes that will expand your knowledge and use of them, while stretching your food budget.

Using your imagination to combine these new foods will lead you to exciting and innovative meals. May you too have the courage to create and expand your gustatory vocabulary.

Acorn Squash Flowers

Sliced acorn squash stuffed with toasted almond rice and served with **Spinach Mint Sauce.**

1	**Acorn Squash**
1 c	**Brown rice**
1/4 c	**Almonds, chopped**
1/2 Tbl	**Soy or tamari**
1 lg	**Garlic clove, pressed**
1/2 c	**Fresh chopped mint**
	Cayenne

Spinach Mint Sauce* see recipe in sauce section

1) Steam the halved seeded squash in a bit of water in a large pot approx. 10-12 minutes. Check with a fork to test firmness (should be firm yet tender—mushy doesn't work). Remove and let cool, then slice into 1″ thick "flowers," skin them, being careful not to lose petal shaped outside. Make sure spines are removed in the valleys between the scalloped part.
2) Cook rice in 2 c water for 30 minutes (Basmati is most fragrant).
3) Toast almonds till lightly brown, and stir soy, garlic, mint and cayenne into rice.
4) Mound rice inside squash "flowers" and bake in a preheated oven 15 minutes at 300-350° till warm.
5) Spoon sauce on bottom of each plate, place a stuffed squash ring on top, sprinkle with mint and serve sauce on side in a gravy server.

Serve with tomato wedges and a crusty bread if desired.

Serves 4

Barbequed Tempeh

1 (8 oz) pk   Tempeh

BBQ Sauce:

1 1/2 Tbl   Natural ketchup
1 Tbl ea.   Honey and onion powder
1 tsp ea.   Tamari and lemon juice
1/4 tsp   Cayenne
1   Garlic clove, pressed
Few drops toasted sesame oil or smoke oil
(brushed on last after cooking)

1) Half and steam tempeh for 10 minutes.
2) Mix sauce together.
3) Brush sauce over both sides of tempeh filets and barbeque or broil for 10 minutes each side.

Serve with corn on the cob and salad or make into tempeh barbeque burgers—add buns and trimmings.

Serves 2

ᴍᴍ Savory Stuffed Zucchini ᴍᴍ

Enjoy your foot long zucchinis with this exotic stuffing. Serve with
Satin Sauce *drizzled on top.*

1 lg	Zucchini, (approx. 1'x4" thick)
2 Tbl (ea)	White wine, lemon juice *and* aminos
1 1/4 c	Celery, finely chopped
1 1/4 c	Onion, chopped
3/4 c	Yellow wax peppers (seed if you don't like "hot")
1 1/4 c	Tomatoes, seeded and chopped
2	Garlic cloves
1/2 c	Sunflower seeds, lightly toasted
1/4 c	Currants
1/2 tsp ea.	Cumin seeds, freshly grated orange peel
1 tsp (ea)	Cumin and coriander powder
1 c	Crumbled firm tofu
	Pinch of sage and seasalt
1 recipe	Satin Sauce

1) Trim ends of zucchini, halve lengthwise and scoop out inner flesh leaving a 1/2" thick shell, sprinkle insides with aminos. Chop flesh and set aside for stuffing. Pre-bake zucchinis at 375° for 25 minutes.

2) Meanwhile make stuffing—heat liquids in deep large skillet on medium, adding veggies and spices in order given. Stir 2 c chopped zucchini flesh, simmer 10-15 minutes.

3) Stuff zucchinis, line cookie sheet with foil, place zucchini on top (pour 1/4 c of water on cookie sheet), and bake at 375° for 45 minutes.

4) Pour warmed sauce on top.

Serves 4

Spinach Tofu Loaf

A healthy meat-less loaf accented with toasted seeds and topped with the **Soygurt Dill Sauce** *below.*

1 lb	Tofu
1 pk	Frozen spinach, chopped
1/4 c	Toasted seeds (sunflower, pinenuts or walnuts)
1/4 c	Fine bread crumbs
1 Tbl ea.	Dill and onion powder
2 tsp	Herbamare or vegetable salt
1/2	Lemon, juiced
2	Garlic cloves
	Dash of Cayenne
1/2 tsp	Lemon pepper

Stir together and place in casserole dish that has been lightly oiled. Sprinkle bread crumbs on top, bake at 375° for 20 minutes.

Soygurt Dill Sauce

1/2 c	Soy yogurt
2 Tbl	Lite mayo or tofunaise
1 tsp ea.	Dill and lemon juice

Whip together and serve on side.

Serves 4-6

Mushroom Seitan in Wine Sauce with Wild Rice

A seductive dish for those desiring a "meaty" taste.

12 oz	Spicy seitan, slice in 1/4″ thick cutlets
1/4 c	Red wine
1/2	Lemon, juiced
1	Garlic clove, minced
2 c	Mushrooms, fresh, sliced

Gravy:

1/2 tsp	Arrowroot powder—mixed with juice from seitan package, stir well

Wild rice (see recipe on page 204)
Parsley as garnish

1) Heat wine, lemon, garlic and mushrooms in skillet, sauté mushrooms till tender. Add gravy, heat and stir.
2) Add seitan, heat till warm.
3) Make a bed of rice on plate, lay seitan slices on top, pour sauce on top.

Serve with a crisp salad or steamed vegetables.

Mushroom Tofu Loaf

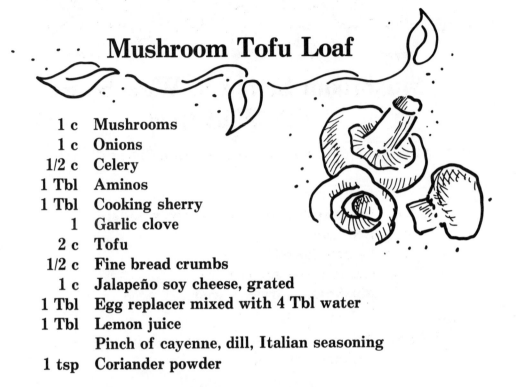

1 c	Mushrooms
1 c	Onions
1/2 c	Celery
1 Tbl	Aminos
1 Tbl	Cooking sherry
1	Garlic clove
2 c	Tofu
1/2 c	Fine bread crumbs
1 c	Jalapeño soy cheese, grated
1 Tbl	Egg replacer mixed with 4 Tbl water
1 Tbl	Lemon juice
	Pinch of cayenne, dill, Italian seasoning
1 tsp	Coriander powder

1) Slice mushrooms, chop onions, mince celery.
2) Sauté in aminos and sherry till tender.
3) Put into medium bowl and add rest of ingredients, stir well. Put into a well oiled baking dish or loaf pan.
4) Bake at 425° for 35 minutes or microwave for 10 minutes with a final broiling of 5 minutes in a toaster oven.

Serve warm with **Mushroom Gravy*** *and a large salad, or chilled with tomato slices.*

*See recipe

Broiled Tofu with Mushrooms

A very tasty layered tofu "Lasagne".

1 lb	Tofu, sliced into 4 sections
1 1/2 c	Mushrooms, sliced

Sauce:

2	Garlic cloves, pressed
1/4 c	Red wine
1/4 c	Liquid aminos
	Cayenne to taste
1/2	Bunch green onions, minced
1/2 Tbl	Chile sesame oil or toasted sesame oil

1) Stir together sauce.
2) Alternate tofu, sauce, mushrooms, sauce etc. in casserole dish.
3) Broil at 450° for 35-45 minutes. Sprinkle green onions on top 15 minutes before done.

Serves 2-3

Roasted Tempeh with Pineapple Salsa

An Indonesian delight, served skewered or baked in a casserole.

8 oz pk	Tempeh
2 Tbl ea	Lemon juice and white wine
1	Garlic clove, pressed
1 tsp	Ginger, pressed
1/4 c	Aminos
1	Bell pepper
1	Onion
	Pineapple salsa—see recipe in sauces

1) Cut tempeh in half, then crossways to create 4 filets—steam 10 minutes.
2) Mix next 4 ingredients and marinate filets for 3 hours or more.
3) Put filets on oiled baking dish, and place slivered onions and peppers around them—or skewer them shishkabob style.

Serves 2-3

Tofu Stuffed Tomatoes

A light, low calorie meal.

4	Tomatoes
1 1/2 c	Tofu, mashed (firm is best)
1/2 c	Minced celery
1/3 c	Onion, minced
1 Tbl	Aminos
1/4 c	Black olives
1 1/2 Tbl	Lemon juice
1/2 tsp ea	Dill weed and onion powder
	Cayenne and gomasio to taste
1 Tbl	Nutritional yeast.

1) Slice top off tomatoes, hollow out, reserve 1/2 c tomato flesh without seeds for stuffing.
2) Sauté onions and celery in aminos till tender.
3) Lightly stir everything together, fill tomatoes.
4) Garnish with sesame seeds or cilantro and serve raw.

Serve with assorted vegetables and sprouts, whole grain toast and parsley garnish.

Serves 4.

Tempeh Cabbage Rolls

*These tasty low-cal rolls go well with steamed whole baby potatoes
and broccoli.*

1 sm ea	**Green and red cabbage**
1	**Onion, minced**
1	**Carrot, minced**
9 oz	**Tempeh cutlet**
2 Tbl ea	**Cooking sherry and red wine**
1/2	**Lemon, juiced**
	To taste: sea salt, black pepper, dill and cumin
	Toasted sesame oil

Sauce:

28 oz	**Crushed Italian tomatoes**
1 tsp	**Dill weed**
1/4 tsp	**Cayenne**
2	**Garlic cloves, pressed**
	Water as needed

1) Heat sherry, wine and lemon juice in heavy skillet, add onion and carrot, cooking on medium heat until soft.
2) Add crumbled tempeh, stir and season to taste—set aside.
3) Steam cabbage whole in a big pot for 10-15 min. until leaves are soft, separate leaves, cut thick rib pieces out.
4) Lay a leaf flat, put a spoonful of filling in center and roll up burrito-style. Place in baking dish, alternate cabbage colors.
5) Stir sauce together, heat gently then pour over rolls, cover and bake at 375° for 40-45 minutes.

Serves 4-6

Bon Temp Tofu Creole

"A whole lotta flavor going on"

1 lb	Tofu, firm, cubed in 1/2" squares
1	Onion, minced
1	Carrot, minced
2	Celery ribs, sliced
2	Garlic cloves, minced
2 Tbl ea.	Aminos, lemon juice
1/2 c	Green peas
2 lg	Green peppers, chop in 1" strips
2	Tomatoes, seeded, chopped
1 c	Tomato sauce
6 oz	Tomato paste with 2 c water
1 Tbl	Cajun spice—see recipe
2 Tbl	Cooking sherry or beer

1) Sauté veggies with amino/lemon mix in a deep heavy skillet till tender.
2) Add spice, tofu and rest of ingredients, stirring all the while.
3) Cook covered for 1 hour on simmer.

Serve over rice or noodles, you can freeze sauce for later use.

Serves 6

Blackened Tofu (or Tempeh)

Marinated Tofu "breaded" with a spicy Cajun seasoning and broiled.
A succulent way to enjoy tofu, also good as a snack or picnic item.
Serve with vegetables.

Preheat oven to Broil 550°

1 lb	**Firm tofu (press between towels to rid tofu of excess water)**
1 Tbl	**Lemon juice (mixed with aminos)**
1 Tbl	**Liquid aminos**
1 1/2 Tbl	**Cajun spice blend—see recipe**

1) Slice tofu into 1/2'' thick filets, then cut each filet crosswise and lenghwise yielding 2″x2″ cutlets. Marinate cutlets in juices minimum of 30 minutes.
2) Put spice blend into a plastic bag and gently shake cutlets to coat evenly.
3) Lay cutlets onto a broiling pan (ventilated so they will get crisp) on top rack of oven. Broil top side 7-9 minutes, turn and broil bottom side 7-9 minutes—or barbeque!

Note: for Tempeh, steam 15 minutes before marinating.

Serves 3-4

Tofu in a Jalapeño Vinaigrette
A hot vinegar marinade gives tofu a sizzle.

8 oz	**Tofu, sliced into 2 thin squares**
2 Tbl	**Cider vinegar**
1 Tbl	**Cooking sherry**
1 Tbl	**Water**
1/2 tsp	**Jalapeño, roasted and diced**
	Pinch of seasalt and cracked black pepper

1) Salt and pepper tofu cutlets, sauté in above mixture on medium high heat, both sides.
2) Transfer to a shallow casserole dish, chill several hours before serving.

Serve on a bed of "Cucumber Pasta"—Cut cucumber into long fine strips. (1/16" wide x 6" long).

Serves 2

Tofu Enchiladas

A creamy tofu filling complements the tasty red chile sauce.

1 dz	Corn tortillas
	Chile Roja Enchilada sauce (see recipe in sauce section)

Filling:

1 1/2 c	Crumbled firm tofu
1 c	Grated soy jalapeño cheese
1/2	Bunch green onions, minced
2	Garlic cloves, pressed
1 tsp ea.	Cumin and onion powder
	Fresh grated nutmeg and peppercorns
	Aminos or dash of sea salt

Topping:

	Sliced black olives
1/2 c	Grated soy cheese
	Thinly sliced onions
	Cilantro leaves

1) Prepare chile sauce (spread a little on the bottom of your baking dish).
2) Mix together the tofu stuffing.
3) Heat tortillas on griddle till soft and warm.
4) Dip into sauce, then place a large spoonful of stuffing horizontally on tortilla and roll up.
5) Do this one at a time, placing on baking dish as you go.
6) Cover with sauce, garnish with last 4 items. Bake 1/2 hour at 350°.

Serves 6

Chile Verde Enchiladas

These enchiladas are stuffed with sauteed squash and tofu cubes and baked in the luscious **Chile Verde Sauce.**

1 lb	Firm tofu
1 c	Yellow squash (pumpkin or butternut)
1 c	Zucchini
1 Tbl	Lemon juice
1	Onion
2	Garlic cloves
1/4 tsp	Nutmeg and black pepper
2 Tbl	Aminos
1 tsp	Oregano
2 dz	Corn tortillas
1 1/2	Soy jack or soy jalapeño cheese
	Chile Verde Sauce—see page 130
	Cilantro as garnish

1) Prepare sauce, have ready.
2) Steam squash till crisp tender not mushy.
3) Cut tofu and squash into 1/2″ cubes. Sauté them with the sliced onions and pressed garlic in lemon juice, aminos and spices. Stir till coated.
4) Heat tortillas on griddle till soft and fill with a heaping spoonful of filling, top with some soy cheese, then roll up and place on a lightly oiled baking dish, cover with sauce.
5) Cover with foil and bake at 375° for 25 minutes, then uncover, lay rest of soy cheese on top and bake uncovered for 10 minutes.

These make good leftovers, or can be frozen.
Serves 8-10

Tempeh Burritos

A very easy dish, make filling ahead and reheat.

Basic:

1/2	Lemon, juiced
1 tsp	Liquid aminos
1 Tbl	Water
6 oz	Cubed tempeh (plain or marinated)
1 lg	Garlic clove, pressed
1	Jalapeño, seeded and chopped
30 oz	Refried beans (vegetarian) or 3 1/2 c of your own
1 tsp	Cumin powder or crushed cumin seeds
1 pk	Favorite soft tortillas
2	Tomatoes, seeded and chopped
1/2 Tbl	Chile powder

1) Heat liquids in saucepan on med/high.
2) Add garlic, Jalapeño and tempeh, stir continuously for 5 minutes.
3) Add rest of seasonings and beans, stir well and simmer.
4) Heat up tortillas in oven or on griddle till soft and warm, fill up with filling, put in baking dish or individual serving dishes, keep warm in oven.

Burrito Options

Pour enchilada sauce on top, cover with grated soy cheese, olives, and green onions; bake 20 minutes at 450°. Or, let everyone make and stuff their own by supplying dishes of:

• Shredded lettuce or cabbage
• Grated soy cheese
• Tomatoes
• Avocados or guacamole

Serves 5-6

Tomatillo Enchilada Casserole

A circular layered enchilada, slice like a pie.

1 dz	Corn tortillas

8 oz	Cactus salsa or Chile Verde Sauce*
1 lb	Tofu
1 c	Jalapeño soy cheese, grated
2	Green onions, chopped
2	Garlic cloves, pressed
1/2	Lemon, juiced
	Vegetable salt, cumin to taste
	Soy Parmesan cheese

1) Blend tofu with next 5 items in food processor or blender.
2) Heat tortillas on griddle till hot, both sides.
3) Layer in a circular casserole baking dish with the salsa on bottom, a tortilla, the filling, another swirl of salsa, a tortilla etc., till all full. Top with soy cheese.
4) Bake at 400° for 25 minutes.

Serves 4, *recipe p. 130*

Tofu Mexicana

A layered Mexican casserole that serves two generously.

8 slices	Tofu, firm (approx. 10 oz.) 1/4″ thickness
1	Green onion, sliced
1 c	Enchilada sauce
2	Tofu pups, sliced
1/4 c	Shredded soy cheddar cheese
1/4 c	Corn kernels
	Garnish with fresh cilantro leaves

1) Pour a bit of sauce into round baking dish.
2) Layer tofu slices, pups, onions, soy cheese, corn, more sauce, tofu slice, etc. till all full. Cover with foil and bake at 425° for 35 minutes or till bubbly.

Chile Rellenos

Hip hip hooray, an eggless dairyless relleno that is delicious!

6	Green Anaheim or California chiles
6	1/2″ strips of soy cheese
1/4 c	Egg replacer mixed with
2/3 c	Water
4 Tbl	Wholewheat pastry flour
1/8 tsp	Turmeric
1/4 tsp	Cumin

Serve with Meximato or Enchilada sauce—see sauce section

1) Wash and dry chiles, put on broiler rack and toast in oven at only 1″ below broiler, turn chiles often so they don't get burned, only blistered and toasted.
2) Put them into a bag to cool, peel carefully when cool.
3) Slice chiles lengthwise, remove pith and seeds and put 1 cheese strip inside (keep stems on for handling and visual presentation)
4) Whip the egg replacer with water till thick, stir in rest of goodies.
5) Place spoonful of coating in heated non stick pan, lay a stuffed chile on top, cover with coating and cook till one side is crisp, then turn gently and cook other side.
6) Keep warm on a plate in the oven at 375° till ready to serve.

Pour **Meximato Sauce** *on top and garnish with cilantro, serve with a side of black beans and a salad.*

Serves 2 generously.

Polenta
with Fennel Tempeh Sauce

A hearty savory meal for hungry eaters.

Polenta:

3 1/4 c	Water
1/2 Tbl	Sea salt
1 c	Course grain corn meal (polenta)
1/3 c	Grated soy Parmesan

Sauce:

2	Fennel bulbs
8 oz	Tempeh
6	Garlic cloves
1 Tbl	Cold pressed vegetable oil of choice
2 Tbl	Wine
8 oz	Mushrooms
1 Tbl	Italian Herbs
2 lg	Tomatoes
6 oz can	Tomato sauce with water to thin
1/2 tsp	Sage

1) Prepare Polenta—bring water to boil, add salt and pour in polenta in a thin stream stirring with a whisk constantly until it begins to thicken at a low heat. Keep stirring for 20 minutes until done, remove from heat, stir in soy cheese.

2) Coarsely chop fennel, mince garlic and sauté in wine and oil with cubed tempeh for 5 minutes.

3) Add 1 c water and cover on low for 15 minutes.

4) Add quartered mushrooms, seeded chopped tomatoes and spices—turn into a sauce by stirring in tomato paste and water.

Serve sauce over polenta, garnish with fennel sprigs.

Serves 4

Pesto Mushroom Manicotti

Mushrooms and pesto blend with soy cheese
for this epicurean medley.

1 lb	Parboiled shells or manicotti
2 lbs	Mushrooms, quartered
1	Onion, chopped
8	Garlic cloves, pressed
4 c	Loose pack basil leaves
1 1/2 Tbl	Aminos
2 tsp	Olive oil
1/4 c	Red wine
	Fresh grated nutmeg and black pepper
4 Tbl	Seasoned bread crumbs
1 c	Soy cheese, grated

1) Sauté mushrooms, onion, garlic in aminos, red wine and oil till tender.
2) Transfer to a food processor and pulse chop till pureed, add basil and rest of ingredients until just mixed.
3) Stuff shells and arrange on a baking dish with a bit of sauce* on bottom, covering with sauce on top, cover with foil and bake 30 minutes at 375°.

*Serve with **Pinenut Bechamel Sauce** or **Tomato Vegetable Cream Sauce** or just your favorite marinara.*

Serves 4-6

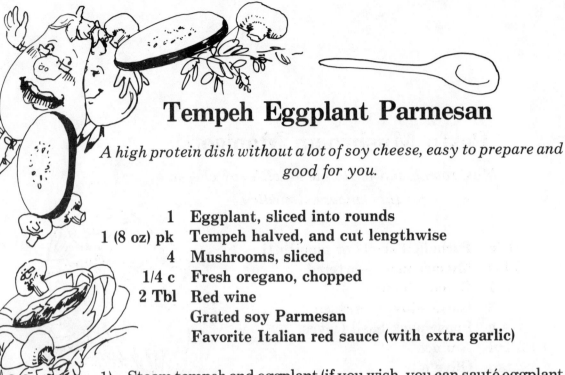

Tempeh Eggplant Parmesan

A high protein dish without a lot of soy cheese, easy to prepare and good for you.

1	Eggplant, sliced into rounds
1 (8 oz) pk	Tempeh halved, and cut lengthwise
4	Mushrooms, sliced
1/4 c	Fresh oregano, chopped
2 Tbl	Red wine
	Grated soy Parmesan
	Favorite Italian red sauce (with extra garlic)

1) Steam tempeh and eggplant (if you wish, you can sauté eggplant in 1 Tbl olive oil and garlic). Preheat oven to 400°.
2) Put red wine in a baking dish and layer in the following order: eggplant, oregano, soy parmesan, sauce, tempeh, mushrooms, soy parmesan, oregano, sauce, eggplant, until all the ingredients are used. Reserve enough red sauce for the top, which is then followed by another grating of soy parmesan and a pretty garnish of 3 mushroom slices. Make it your masterpiece!
3) Bake for 25 minutes at 400° or so, till heated thru.

Serve with large salad, spinach is nice; or on a platter of polenta.

Serves 4

Pesto Pasta

Fragrant basil makes a delicious sauce for fresh pasta.

1 lb	**Pasta, fresh is best**
1	**Recipe Pesto Sauce**
2-3 Tbl	**Hot water (from pasta)**
2 Tbl	**Toasted pine nuts**
	Extra Soy Parmesan for top

1) Cook pasta al dente, drain
2) Spoon water into pesto to thin and stir into pasta.
3) Garnish with nuts and soy parmesan cheese.

Serves 4 generously

Marinara Love Sauce over Spaghetti Squash

A favorite vegetable sauce, served over steaming squash "pasta" in its own shell.

Sauce:

1	Onion
4 Tbl	Red wine (chianti)
1 tsp	Olive oil
2	Garlic cloves
1	Bell pepper, diced
1 c	Mushrooms, sliced
28 oz	Crushed tomatoes
1/4 tsp	Crushed red chile flakes and cracked black pepper
1/2 tsp ea	Crushed fennel seeds and Basil (or use a fresh sprig)
2 Tbl	Grated soy Parmesan

1) Heat 2 Tbl wine and oil in large skillet on medium heat. Add onions, garlic, peppers—stirring gently till tender.
2) Stir in tomatoes, mushrooms, herbs and wine, let simmer.
3) After 1/2 hr., stir in soy cheese, salt, pepper, and more water if necessary. Meanwhile prepare squash recipe on next page.

Serves 2-4

Squash:

> 1 lg   **Spaghetti squash**
> 1 Tbl   **Grated Soy Parmesan cheese**
>   **Fresh grated nutmeg and black pepper to taste**

1) Prick squash with fork and bake 30 minutes or until shell is tender in 350° oven.
2) Split shell in half when cool, scoop out seeds, discard, then scoop out flesh into a bowl (reserve shells).
3) Mix squash with rest of ingredients, keep warm in oven.
4) Spoon 1/2 of squash into each 1/2 of shell, spoon sauce on top. Serve. Garnish with a parsley sprig.

Okra Curry

A tasty vegetable curry served over Basmati rice.

12 or so	**Okras**
1	**Leek**
1	**Carrot**
2	**Potatoes**
4	**Garlic cloves**
1 Tbl	**Curry**
1 tsp ea.	**Cumin seeds and dill**
2 tsp ea.	**Coriander and Tamari**
2 Tbl	**Cooking sherry**
	Water to cover (approx. 1-2 cups)
	Dash of cayenne

1) Chop and slice all veggies.
2) Put in pan with garlic and spices (use your own feeling with using spices)
3) Cover with water. Bring to boil, reduce to simmer and cover for 20 min. or so.

Serve with Basmati rice, and **Cucumbermint Raita.**

Serves 3

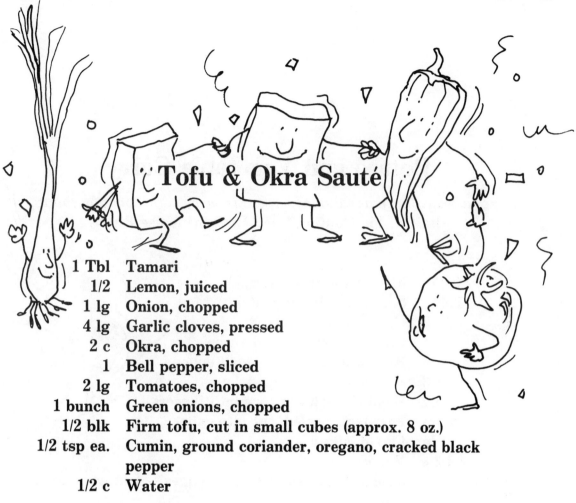

Tofu & Okra Sauté

1 Tbl	Tamari
1/2	Lemon, juiced
1 lg	Onion, chopped
4 lg	Garlic cloves, pressed
2 c	Okra, chopped
1	Bell pepper, sliced
2 lg	Tomatoes, chopped
1 bunch	Green onions, chopped
1/2 blk	Firm tofu, cut in small cubes (approx. 8 oz.)
1/2 tsp ea.	Cumin, ground coriander, oregano, cracked black pepper
1/2 c	Water

1) In a large skillet, heat tamari and lemon juice, add onions and garlic, toss, add okra and peppers, continue to sauté 5 minutes.
2) Add tofu and rest of ingredients, cover with water.
3) Simmer on low till veggies are cooked, approximately one half hour, stir occasionally.

Serve over **Yellow Rice**. *(see recipe in grain section)*

Serves 2-4

Potato and Vegetable Curry

For a beautiful Indian dinner serve this curry with **Cucumbermint Raita*, Fig Chutney*** *and* **Basmati Anise Rice***

2 1/2 Tbl	Master curry (see recipe)
1 Tbl ea	Safflower oil and water
2	Garlic cloves, pressed
1	Onion, quartered and sliced
4	Red potatoes cut in small cubes
2	Bell peppers, chopped
1/2	Head Cauliflower torn into flowers
1 sm	Eggplant, peeled, cut into cubes
1 lg	Carrot, sliced
2 1/2 c	Water
	3 roma tomatoes cut into wedges — Add when done

1) Heat oil and water in pan, add curry stirring until bubbly.
2) Add aminos, stir around 5 min., add rest of vegetables.
3) Pour water over and cover for 20 min. or so, till tender, stir in tomatoes last minute.

Serves 3-4

*See page 152, 153, and 205 respectively.

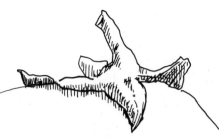

Eggplant Bean Threads

Woked vegetables seasoned with
sherry and ginger nestled in clear noodles.

1 pk	Bean thread noodles (about 4 oz.)
3 Tbl	Soy sauce
1 tsp	Honey
1/4 tsp	Grated ginger
	Few drops toasted sesame oil
1	Eggplant
1 bunch	Green onions
3	Celery ribs
3 Tbl	Cooking sherry
1 Tbl	Aminos
1 c	Shelled green peas
1	Tomato
1/2 c	Water

1) Rinse and soak the bean thread noodles in warm water, 10 min. or so. Gently boil till tender in a pot of water, this will only take a few minutes, drain.
2) Combine next 4 ingredients and toss into noodles.
3) Peel and slice eggplant into bite size pieces, shred onions diagonally, slice celery, seed and chop tomato.
4) Put 1/2 c water in wok and all vegetables, bring to boil, then simmer till crisp tender, stir in noodles, coat well and serve warm.

Serves 2-4

Tempeh in Peanut Sauce

A tempeh "satay" in spicy peanut sauce.

8 oz	**Tempeh**
1 Tbl	**Lemon juice**
1 Tbl	**Tamari**
1/2	**Onion**
1/4 c	**Water**
	Tofu Thai Peanut Sauce—see recipe on page 138
	Bean threads or glass noodles, cooked al dente.

1) Thinly slice onion, chop tempeh.
2) Marinate 1st four ingredients a few hours.
3) Place water in wok, heat up, add tempeh and marinade, cook 15 minutes or until done.
4) Stir in peanut sauce. Serve over bean thread noodles.

Serve over noodles and with **Thai Bright Salad** *page 88.*

Serves 4

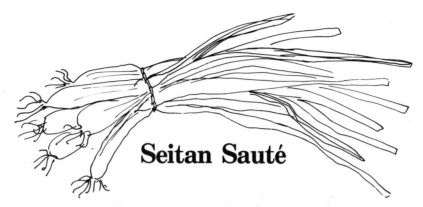

Seitan Sauté

Seasoned seitan* filets combine with woked vegetables, served rolled up in mu-shu pancakes.

1/2	**Lime, juiced**
1/2	**Lemon, juiced**
1 Tbl	**Tamari**
2 Tbl	**Water (or more if you like it "juicy")**
1/2″	**Piece ginger, peeled and chopped**
1 lg	**Garlic clove, pressed**
1	**Jalapeño, seeded, minced (keep seeds in if you like spicy hot foods)**
4	**Zucchinis, chopped**
1/2 lb	**Mushrooms**
1 bunch	**Green onions**
	Spiced Seitan, sliced (figure 2-3 slices per person)
	Mushu pancakes or tortillas
	Ornamental lettuces, fresh tomato wedges and cucumber spears

1) Heat up juices, water and tamari in wok.
2) Add next 3 ingredients, toss well.
3) Add next 3 ingredients, stir and cover for a couple of minutes.
4) Add vegetables, stir another 5 minutes or so.
5) Add seitan slices on top and let steam till warmed, place your pancakes on top to further steam if you want.
6) Garnish each dish or bowl with lettuces around perimeter, fill with woked veggies, place seitan on top, arrange tomatoes and cucumber around edges, serve with warmed pancakes.

Serves 3-4

*see page 15.

Cabbage Noodles for 2

*Woked shredded cabbage and oriental noodles
tossed in a seasoned sauce.*

2	Portions samen, ramen or soba noodles
1/3 c	Water
1/2	Head cabbage
1	Onion
2	Garlic cloves
1/2 Tbl	Mirin or cooking sherry
1 1/2 Tbl	Tamari
1 sm	Bunch Cilantro leaves
	Dash of cayenne

1) Cook noodles al dente, drain.
2) Slice vegetables thinly or shred them.
3) Heat water in wok and add vegetables.
4) Cook on high for 4-5 minutes.
5) Add last 4 items, stir, then throw in noodles and toss well.
6) Transfer to a serving platter.

Serves 2-3

Serve with **Ginger Longbeans,** *see recipe.*

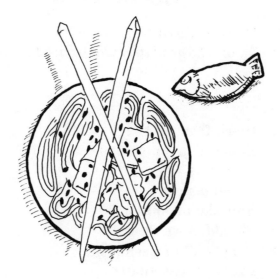

Tofu Marinade Over Daikon Shreds

A marvelous light meal with a Japanese flair.

1 lb	Tofu, sliced
1/4 c	Mirin or sake
1/4 c	Tamari
1/2 Tbl	Minced ginger root
1 tsp	Honey
1 c	Daikon, shredded
1/4 c	Yellow squash, shredded
1 c	Lettuce, shredded

1) Blend sauce and pour over tofu slices, arrange on a flat tray, refrigerate overnight.
2) Heat gently, or top broil as is, or use this crust: Mix together: 3 Tbl roasted ground sesame seeds and 2 Tbl flour (whole grain), sauté in aminos until browned.
3) Lay tofu on top of the shredded veggies, serve.

Serves 2-4

Mushu Tofu

A delectable Chinese burrito, served with a spicy dipping sauce.
Serve the stir fry on a large platter along with the steamed pancakes.

1/2	Block firm tofu
1 1/2	Bunches green onions
3	Zucchinis
1	Green pepper
5	Shiitake mushrooms
1 1/2 c	Shredded woodears*
1 Tbl	Canola oil or peanut oil
1 Tbl	Fresh grated ginger
1/4 tsp	Toasted sesame oil
2 Tbl	Tamari
1 tsp	(ea.) Mirin and honey
1 pk	Mushu pancakes
	Hoisin Sauce* or Mushu sauce

1) Cut tofu into thin strips, mince onions, slice thin zucchinis and pepper.
2) Soak dried mushrooms and woodears in water till soft, discard stems, then slice.
3) Heat oil and tamari in wok, add zucchinis and peppers, stir to coat. Then add tofu, mushrooms and ginger, and after 3 minutes add the onions and woodears.
4) Pour mirin and honey on top stir quickly to coat evenly.
5) Serve rolled into hot pancakes, roll like a burrito with the ends folded, serve with sauce if desired.

*Available in oriental markets.

Serves 4

Pineapple Soba Tempehtation

A sweet and sour tempeh stir fry with noodles

1 (8 oz) pk	**Tempeh**
1	**Red onion**
2 lg	**Bell peppers**
1 c	**Pineapple**
2	**Tomatoes, seeded**
1 Tbl	**Aminos**
1 (8 oz) pk	**Soba noodles**
1 tsp	**Toasted sesame oil**

Marinade

2 lg	**Garlic cloves, pressed**
1″	**Piece fresh ginger, minced**
2 tsp	**Apple cider vinegar**
	Dash of Cayenne

1) Chop tempeh in cubes, stir together marinade, marinate in sauce overnight or a few hours before preparation.
2) Cook soba in boiling water till al dente, strain and set aside.
3) Slice onions, chop peppers, pineapple and tomatoes.
4) Heat aminos in wok, sauté onion, add tempeh and a bit of water, stir continuously.
5) Add peppers and stir, then add soba, and rest of veggies—turn off heat when veggies are still crisp.
6) Stir in sesame oil last—serve hot.

Serves 2-3

Thai Vegetable Sauté

Coconut and peanut flavor this exotic spicy sauté.

1 lg	Red bell pepper
(15 oz) can	Baby corn
10 med	Mushrooms
1 sm	Red onion
2 lg	Garlic cloves
1 Tbl	Aminos
1	Lemon, juiced
1/2 c	Coconut milk
1/4 c	Peanut butter
1/2 Tbl	Tamari
	Dash of red chile flakes and cayenne
	Ginger, pressed
	Water to thin

1) Slice peppers, mushrooms and onion.
2) Press garlic into wok with lemon juice and aminos, sauté.
3) Add rest of veggies, stir till crisp-cooked.
4) Stir last 4 ingredients together, add water if necessary, pour over vegetables, stir to coat.

Serve with jasmine rice or couscous—If tofu or tempeh is desired, cube and marinate in coconut sauce a few hours before adding to vegetable sauté.

Serves 2-4

Wonton in Kombu Broth

*These heavenly wontons are much too easy to eat,
be careful not to over cook.*

1/2 lb	Firm tofu, crumbled
2 lg	Garlic cloves, pressed
1″ piece	Ginger, minced (fresh)
1/2 tsp	Lemon rind, grated
1 Tbl	Soy sauce
1 oz	Kombu (1 strip)
2 qts	Water
1 bunch	Green onions (1 packed cup)
1 can	Water chestnuts (8 oz.)
1/2 tsp	Toasted sesame oil
	A couple of threads of saffron
1 pk	Wonton wrappers

1) Marinate top 5 ingredients overnight.
2) Prepare broth; put washed kombu in water, bring to boil and cook on medium heat for 1/2 hr.
3) Meanwhile make wonton stuffing: put green onions, water chestnuts, oil and saffron into a blender or food processor, pulse chop several seconds. Add marinated tofu, chop till a paste-like consistency forms.
4) Fill each wonton square with 1 heaping tsp. of filling, seal edges with water, fold into a triangle, twist edges, right over left and seal with more water
5) Strain out kombu, bring back to a boil.
6) Add wontons to boiling broth, cook a couple of minutes then strain out. These cook very quickly, eyes open!
7) Pour broth into separate bowls, add a few wontons, garnish with minced chives or cilantro.

Serves 4

Tofu in Vegetable Nests

Hot tofu nestled in cool shredded baskets—a surprising combination.

Nests:

2	Carrots
1/4	Cabbage
2	Celery ribs
1 Tbl	Rice vinegar
	Sesame oil, few drops

Tofu:

1/2 blk	Tofu, diced
1/4 c	Peas
2 Tbl	Mirin
1 Tbl	Lemon juice
1/2 Tbl	Tamari

Buckwheat sprouts
Sunflower sprouts

1) Finely shred vegetables for nests, toss with vinegar and oil.
2) Sauté tofu and peas in juices with liquids till hot and tender.
3) Assemblage: press vegetables into nests in separate bowls, scoop tofu into nests. Surround with long sprouts forming a ring.

Eat with chop sticks.

Serves 2

Pasta Exotica

This delicious pasta uses lotus roots, baby corn and tofu woked with simmered greens. The sweet and spicy glaze works great over fresh pastas. Add whatever vegetables or flowers you wish and amaze your guests!

1 pk	Marinated tofu cake (approx. 10 oz)*
1 pk	Lotus root, boiled (approx. 5.2 oz)*
15oz can	Baby corn
6 c	Shredded greens, packed (bokchoy, chard, etc.)
1 Tbl	Tamari
2 Tbl	Aminos
	Red chili flakes and toasted sesame seeds, a couple of drops toasted sesame oil
1 lb	Pasta, fresh (try flavored kinds like red cajun tomato, jalapeño etc.)
1	Recipe Wok Glaze (prepared ahead of time)
2	Tomatoes

1) Marinate tofu slices, lotus and corn in tamari.
2) Cook pasta al dente and keep covered on side.
3) Heat wok, add aminos and tofu marinade mixture, stir, then cover for a minute.
4) Add greens, cover to steam a couple minutes, then sprinkle red chili flakes and sesame seeds on top, stir well to mix.
5) Pour glaze into vegetables, toss to coat evenly, add toasted sesame oil—turn off heat.
6) Put pasta on a serving platter, mix in vegetables and garnish with fresh tomato wedges in pattern.

Serves 3-4.

*Available in Oriental groceries.

Tempeh with Vegetables

Serves 2 hungry eaters.

1/4 c	Cooking sherry
2 Tbl	Lemon or lime juice
1 Tbl	Safflower oil
1 (8oz) pk	Tempeh, cubed and steamed 10 minutes
1/2 dz pk	Fresh oyster mushrooms
1 lg	Green pepper
1/4 tsp	Roasted sesame oil
2 Tbl	Shoyu or Tamari
1/4 c	Water
1 Tbl	Cilantro leaves
1 lg	Tomato

1) Heat sherry, oil and lemon juice in wok, add garlic and tempeh. Stir on high heat till tempeh begins to brown.
2) Add green pepper, stir for 3 minutes, add rest of ingredients (except tomato and cilantro). Continue stirring till tender for 5 or so minutes.
3) Add tomato, stir again and turn off heat. Cover.
4) Toss in cilantro before serving.

Serve with couscous or rice pilaf (many tasty instant rice-like dishes are available for when you have no time.)

No Soba Soba

The parsnip resembles pasta in this all veggie, nicely spiced stirfry.

1 Tbl	Tamari
1/4 c	Lemon juice
2 Tbl	Mirin (cooking sake)
1 big	Parsnip, peeled and cut into 3" or 4" sections, then slice into thin pasta-like strips
1/4 head	Red cabbage, chopped
1/2	Eggplant, cubed and skinned
1" piece	Ginger
1/4 c	Water
8	Shiitake mushrooms (fresh if possible)
1 bunch	Spinach, sliced
4	Garlic cloves, minced
1/2 lb	Tofu, firm, cut into 1/2" cubes
Dash	Cayenne
	Sesame seeds as garnish

1) Put first 3 liquids in hot wok, add parsnip "pasta", cabbage and eggplant, stir and cover on med-hi heat, cook 10 minutes, stir occasionally.

2) Meanwhile put ginger in blender with water, blend then add to wok.

3) Add rest of items, heat gently, stir to coat and serve with rice.

Serves 2

Eggplant Nori Rolls

These are very easy to make, especially if you already have rice cooked from last night's meal. Try different types of rice for variation.

1 1/2 c	**Cooked short grain sushi rice***
3	**Eggplant slices**
	Nori sheets
1 Tbl	**Water**
2 Tbl	**Mirin**
	Squeeze of lemon
1 tsp	**(ea.) Ginger and tamari**
1/4 tsp	**Toasted sesame oil**
	Gomasio or toasted sesame seeds
	Wasabi and tamari as condiments

1) Cut each eggplant slice into 1/2" thick strips.
2) Heat water, add mirin and lemon to skillet or wok—add minced fresh ginger, tamari and eggplant, stir while cooking a few minutes only, then turn off heat.
3) Add sesame oil, stir.
4) Take nori sheet, lay a bed of rice over it covering 3/4 of sheet. Lay eggplant strips horizontally down center, sprinkle with gomasio, then carefully roll up using both hands. Seal edges with water.
5) Slice nori rolls and arrange on a platter. Serve with a dipping sauce of wasabi paste and tamari in individual bowls.

*See recipe in grain section. Makes four nori rolls.

DESSERTS

DESSERTS

My passionate sweet tooth has inspired a great deal of experimentation to find healthy, nutritious, low calorie desserts that could truly satisfy.

Imagine eating chocolate mousse, cake and ice cream; all without dairy products, eggs, butter, refined sugar and flour. The recipes herein include refreshing and nonfattening mousses, puddings, parfaits, fruit sorbets and gels which are a perfect fulfillment to any meal.

Then there are a few cake, pie and torte recipes to intoxicate even the most spirited sweet tooth.

Go ahead and indulge in these enlightening desserts and taste a new level of sweetness in your life.

Fresh Fruit Desserts

Begin substituting fresh colorful juicy fruits as a dessert. It will quench your sweet tooth and is so much better for you, leaving you with a light (rather than stuffed) feeling after a wonderful meal.

Light and luscious dairyless desserts

Banana Ice Cream

The first all fruit ice cream I ever made, one bite and I was addicted.

2 **Bananas, frozen, chopped**

1) Blend or puree in a food processor.
2) Stop and stir till thick and creamy, serve immediately.

Serves one

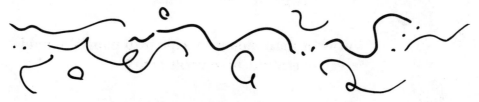

Cocoa Banana Ice Cream

1/2 lb **Soft tofu**
2 c **Frozen bananas**
1/4 c **Cocoa powder**
1/4 c **Fructose or sweetener of choice**

Blend in food processor till creamy, refreeze 2 hours for extra icyness.

Serves 2

Chocolate Mousse

The silken tofu is the key to a light mousse.

1 pk	Silken soft tofu
1/3 c	Maple syrup or honey
2 Tbl	Cocoa powder
1 tsp	Vanilla extract
1 tsp	Peanut butter (optional)

Puree till smooth, refrigerate or freeze 2 hours before use.

Fudgesicles

A great treat for kids!

Put chocolate mousse recipe into popsicle molds—freeze overnight or several hours.

Chocolate Mint Mousse

Follow chocolate mousse recipe and add:

1/4 tsp	Peppermint extract
	Garnish with a mint leaf

Serves 3-4

Raspberry Bavarian Mousse

Very easy to make and delicious, too!

1 pk   Silken tofu (10.5 oz)
1/4 c   Natural Raspberry syrup
3/4 c   Raspberries (frozen)
1/4 tsp   Almond extract
1/2 tsp   Vanilla extract

Puree till creamy, freeze 1-2 hours before serving.

Serves 3-4

Strawberry Mousse

To above recipe substitute strawberries instead of raspberry, use strawberry jam as a sweetener.

Raspberry Cocoa Mousse

1 pk   Silken tofu
2 Tbl   Natural Raspberry syrup
2 Tbl   Cocoa powder
1 Tbl   Honey
1/4 c   Frozen raspberries

Puree in food processor, freeze 2 hours or refrigerate overnight—garnish with fresh raspberries or a mint leaf.

Fresh Fruit Ices

Bananas, strawberries, peaches, apricots, or any frozen fruit creates a refreshing dessert or afternoon treat.

Freeze berries or fruit of choice, put into a food processor or blender. Blend till smooth, adding enough juice to blend. Serve immediately or, freeze 1 hour to firm up before serving.

Purple Passion

A cooling treat.

1/2 c	(4 oz.) Tofu, soft
1-1/2 c	Frozen blueberries
2 Tbl	Honey or natural fruit syrup
	Few drops peppermint oil or extract

Blend all till smooth—great after fiery spicy foods.

Piña Colada Sorbet

A tropical lo-cal sorbet.

2 c	Pineapple chunks
1	Banana
1/4 c	Pineapple coconut juice or orange juice

1) Freeze pineapple overnight.
2) Blend or puree with banana, adding juice slowly. Stop and stir till it is all pureed—put into glasses or dessert cups and freeze 1 hr. before serving.

Serves 4

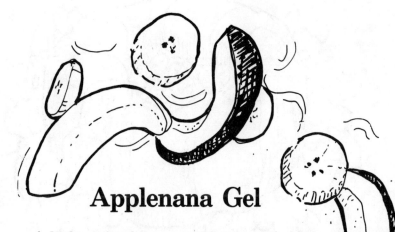

Applenana Gel

A light refreshing apple-banana dessert.

3 c	Apple juice
1 Tbl	Agar flakes
1 c	Vanilla soy yogurt
2 Tbl	Maple syrup
1	Banana
1	Anna apple
	Sprinkle of clove and cinnamon

1) Whisk agar into 1/2 c apple juice.
2) Heat rest of apple juice (including agar mixture) in small sauce pan till boiling. Reduce heat, stir in spices and syrup, continue cooking on low for 3-5 minutes, when cool, stir in soy yogurt.
3) Slice fruit, put inside a 4-cup mold.
4) Pour cooled juice on top—chill in freezer for 4 hours.

Serves 4

Fresh Fruit Ring

A beautiful Low-cal fresh fruit mold.

2	Baskets of sweet fresh strawberries, sliced
2	Peaches, sliced
6 oz	Fresh fruit smoothie (or 1 3/4 c juice blended with 2 very ripe or frozen bananas)
1/8 c	Coconut shredded
1 1/2 tsp	Agar
1/2 c	Water

1) Mix water and agar. Bring to a boil with some of the juice—stir and simmer.
2) Put sliced fruit in bowl—pour in rest of juice and agar—mix thoroughly.
3) Pour into decorative ring and chill in freezer 1 1/2 hours, then serve—or refrigerate several hours. Invert onto a pretty crystal or glass plate, decorate with flowers or sliced fruit.

Serves 4

Fruity Vanilla Parfait

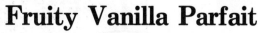

Layer one, red:

1 c	**Frozen fruit of choice (raspberries, strawberries)**
2 Tbl	**Natural fruit syrup**
1/4 c	**Vanilla soy yogurt**

Layer two, white, yellow or green:

1 c	**Fresh frozen fruit of choice (kiwis, bananas, peaches or apricots)**
1/2 c	**Vanilla soy yogurt**
1 tsp	**Vanilla extract**
1 Tbl	**Honey or fruit syrup**

Topping:

Vanilla or fruit soy yogurt drizzled with fruit syrup and fresh fruit spears or berries.

1) Blend 1st group, spoon into small parfait glasses or champagne flutes put in a freezer for 1-2 hours.
2) Blend 2nd group and spoon on top. Chill in freezer 2 hours.
3) Let thaw 1/2 hour before serving, top with goodies.

Makes 3-4 servings

Amazake Carob Pudding

A naturally sweetened cultured rice drink that makes a quick and easy rice dessert.

16 oz   **Amazake**
1 Tbl   **Carob powder**
1 Tbl   **Arrowroot powder and water to thin**
        Toasted almond slivers for garnish
        Honey, if desired

1)   Gently heat amazake in small pan.
2)   Mix arrowroot with water, add to amazake.
3)   Whisk in carob, heat until thick, pour into dessert glasses or wine glasses, chill a few hours before serving. Top with nuts.

Serves 3

Tofu Flan

A silky custard with hints of orange and lemon, baked in a carmelized syrup. It is best served chilled, complementary to spicy foods.

Caramel:

1/2 c	**Fructose**
3 Tbl	**Water**
1/2 tsp	**Vanilla extract**
1/4 tsp	**Almond extract**

Custard:

30 oz	**Silken soft tofu (2 packs)**
1 tsp	**Vanilla extract**
1 Tbl	**Orange Liqueur (triple sec is good)**
1 tsp	**Lemon peel, grated**
1/2 c	**Fresh squeezed Orange juice**
2 tsp	**Agar flakes**

1) Pre-heat oven to 350°
2) Combine caramel ingredients in a small heavy saucepan, stir and cook over med. heat until amber colored, no more than 5 minutes total.
3) Pour into dry muffin tins and set aside.
4) Puree custard ingredients (except for O.J. and agar) in food processor. Stir agar into O.J. and bring to a boil for one minute in a small sauce pan, stir into custard and pour into muffin tins.
5) Place muffin tins into a larger pan and fill outer pan with 1″ depth of water (so muffin tin "floats" in water).
6) Bake 30 minutes, cool 2 hrs. before serving. To invert flan, loosen with a knife along perimeter of cups.

Silken Orange Carrot Pie

*A light delicious pie with a gorgeous orange color and the fragrance
of spicy orange blossoms.*

2 c	Carrots, pureed
3/4 c	Fresh orange juice
2 Tbl	Agar flakes
1 Tbl	Arrowroot powder
10.5 oz pk	Silken tofu
1 tsp	grated orange rind
1/4 tsp	Cardamon, fresh ground
	Dash of each cinnamon and clove powder
1	Recipe Granola Pie Crust, page 296

1) Chop and cook carrots until soft—puree
2) Mix O.J. with agar and arrowroot, bring to a boil in a small
   sauce pan, stir for 1 minute until thick, then set aside.
3) Add tofu, spices and O.J. mix to carrots, and puree in food
   processor.
4) Pour into pie crust, chill several hours or overnight until set.

*Serve with **Sauce of Angels** or vanilla soy ice cream if desired.*

Serves 6-8

Cocoa Berry Cream Pie

A luscious low fat dessert that is best served quite chilled. Blueberries enliven this dairyless cocoa pie.

2 c	"Lite" cocoa soy milk
1/4 c	Agar flakes
1 tsp	Vanilla extract
1 Tbl	Carob powder
3 Tbl	Maple syrup
1 Tbl	Arrowroot powder
1 1/2 c	Blueberries (fresh or frozen)

1) Whisk first 6 items together in a medium sauce pan on high heat until boiling. Simmer and stir a few more minutes until thick.
2) Stir in blueberries and pour into Almondine Crust. Refrigerate till firm, at least 2-4 hours before serving.

Almondine Crust

A wonderful crust of soaked almonds.

1 c	Almonds (soaked in water overnight, minimum 10 hrs.)
1/4 c	Raisins
3 Tbl	Whole wheat pastry flour
1 Tbl	Peanut butter
dash	Cinnamon

1) Drain almonds and grind all together in a food processor.
2) Press into a pie pan and bake in a preheated oven at 400° for 15 minutes. Fill and chill.

Serves 6-8

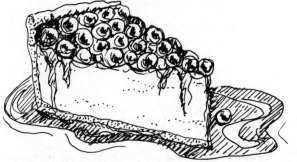

Blueberry Almondine "Cheesecake"

A luscious non-dairy, tofu pie with grated lemon peel and fresh blueberries, top it with the blueberry glaze.

10.5 oz	Silken soft tofu
8.5 oz.	Lite vanilla soy milk (1 1/2 c)
1/4 c	Agar flakes
2 Tbl	Honey
1/4 tsp	Almond extract
1/2 tsp	Grated lemon rind (organic)
1 1/4 c	Fresh blueberries

1) Blend (all except berries) in processor or blender until silky.
2) Transfer to a med. pot and bring to rolling boil (on med.-hi heat), stirring constantly with a whisk, set aside to cool down a bit.
3) Pour into Almond crust, let sit a few minutes, put blueberries on top and refrigerate.

Almond Crust

1 c	Soaked almonds
1/4 c	Raisins
1/2 Tbl	Peanut butter
1/4 c	Oatbran
1/4 tsp	Almond extract

Grind, press into shallow quiche dish, bake 15 minutes at 375° in a preheated oven.

Serves 6

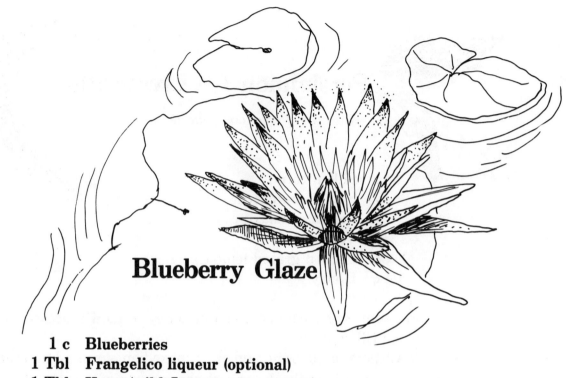

Blueberry Glaze

1 c	Blueberries
1 Tbl	Frangelico liqueur (optional)
1 Tbl	Kuzu (wild Japanese arrowroot)
2 Tbl	Water
1 c	Fruit juice (apple, raspberry, etc.)

1) Wash berries, set aside.
2) Dissolve kuzu in water, put in to small pan with juice. Bring to boil stirring constantly, turn to low heat and cook until mixture thickens, just a couple minutes.
3) Stir in berries, simmer a few more minutes. Serve hot over "cheesecake".

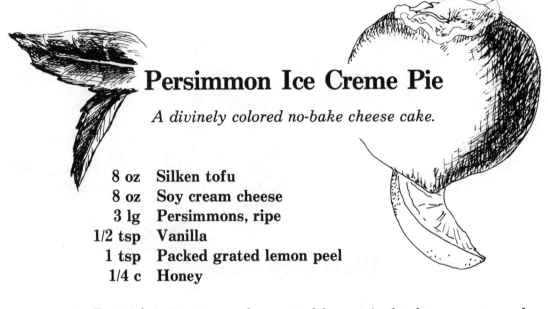

Persimmon Ice Creme Pie

A divinely colored no-bake cheese cake.

8 oz	Silken tofu
8 oz	Soy cream cheese
3 lg	Persimmons, ripe
1/2 tsp	Vanilla
1 tsp	Packed grated lemon peel
1/4 c	Honey

1) Put tofu, soy cream cheese, and honey in food processor and blend till smooth.
2) Mash persimmons and add other ingredients, stir all together.
3) Pour into pie shell—I suggest the granola pie crust below.
4) Freeze for several hours, until set.

Let thaw 1 1/2 hours before serving.

Granola Pie Crust

Raw!

2 c	Granola, (finely ground in blender)
1-1/2 Tbl	Melted soy margarine
1/8 c	Barley malt or rice syrup

1) Stir all together and press into fluted dish or pie pan.

Pear Custard Cream Pie

A dairyless custard pudding makes a great base
for fresh sliced ripe pears.

5-6	Ripe pears
1	Lemon
1 1/2 c	Creamy soy milk
2 tsp	Fructose
2 Tbl	Arrowroot powder or Kuzu
1 Tbl	Agar
1	Pastry crust, pre-baked page 300
2 Tbl	Dark chocolate, melted, thin with 1 Tbl water

1) Skin, core and slice pears. Put them into a bowl and toss with lemon juice and fructose.
2) Mix arrowroot and agar with 1/4 c soy milk till smooth, then transfer to a heavy pot, adding rest of soy milk, heat on med. Stir until mixture thickens. Mix 1/2 of pears into custard.
3) Grate peel from lemon, stir into custard. Melt chocolate.
4) Now assemble: put custard on bottom, arrange pears on top, drizzle chocolate fancifully, chill for several hours before serving.

Serves 6

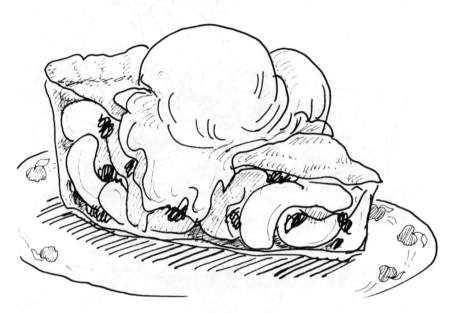

Apple Pie

A hearty and spicy pie, delicious with vanilla soy ice cream.

3 lg	Apples, skinned, cored, sliced thin
2 Tbl	Wholewheat pastry flour
1/2	Lemon, juiced
1/4 c	Raisins, soaked (monukahs are best)
	Drizzle of maple syrup
	Gratings of fresh nutmeg
	Cinnamon
1/4 c	Granola (maple is good)
1	Pastry crust, page 300

1) Prepare apples, pre-bake pie shell (6 min., 375°).
2) Squeeze lemon over apples in medium size bowl, toss with rest of ingredients.
3) Grind granola in blender. Fill pie crust with apples. Sprinkle on granola and bake until brown—approx. 25-30 min. at 350°.

Serves 6

Tropical Rice Pudding

A sweet and chewey rice delight.

2 c	Water
1 c	Sweet brown rice
2 c	Vanilla soy milk
1 c	Pineapple chunks
1/2 c	Coconut, lightly toasted
1/4 c	Dried papaya diced
2 Tbl	Egg replacer beaten stiff with 8 Tbl water
1	Banana, sliced
1 tsp	Rum extract (optional)
1 Tbl	Apple concentrate or sweetener of choice

1) Bring water to a near boil, add rice, stir and cover, turn to simmer, cook 35 minutes, turn off heat.
2) Add fruits, soy milk, fold in egg replacer mixture, put into an oiled baking dish. Bake 350° for 30-40 minutes.

Serves 4-6

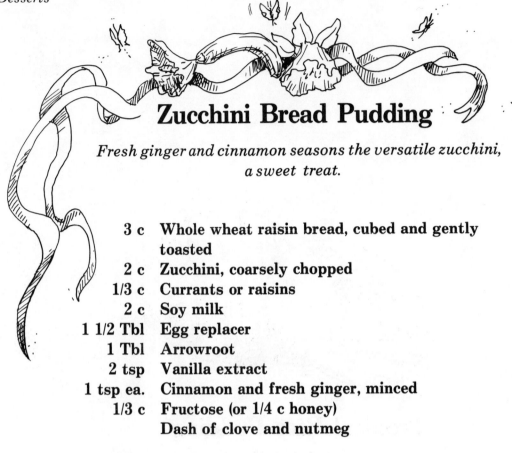

Zucchini Bread Pudding

Fresh ginger and cinnamon seasons the versatile zucchini,
a sweet treat.

3 c	Whole wheat raisin bread, cubed and gently toasted
2 c	Zucchini, coarsely chopped
1/3 c	Currants or raisins
2 c	Soy milk
1 1/2 Tbl	Egg replacer
1 Tbl	Arrowroot
2 tsp	Vanilla extract
1 tsp ea.	Cinnamon and fresh ginger, minced
1/3 c	Fructose (or 1/4 c honey)
	Dash of clove and nutmeg

1) Toss first 3 items in large bowl.
2) Blend soy milk with rest of goodies, pour over bread mixture, toss gently and pour into a baking dish and bake for 1 hour at 375°.

Serves 4

Pastry Crust

1/3 c	Soy margarine
1 1/2 c	Wholewheat pastry flour
1/2	Lemon, juiced (1 tbl)
1/3 c	Walnuts, finely ground

1) Cut in soy margarine with rest of ingredients—using a fork (or pulse chop in food processor just until thick). Add 1 - 2 Tbl of ice water, as needed.
2) Press evenly into a pie crust, work from center of pan out. Prebake at 375° for 5 minutes, let cool then fill with fruit or filling of choice.

Brandy Orange Cake

A moist and luscious no oil, no egg cake, layered with a light **Tofu Orange Creme Frosting** *(see next page).*

1 tsp	Curacao (orange liqueur)
2 Tbl	Brandy
2 med	Oranges
2 Tbl	Egg replacer mixed with
1/3 c	Soy yogurt
1/2 c	Honey
1 tsp	Vanilla
3 Tbl	Turbinado or date sugar
1 1/2 c	Wholewheat pastry flour
2 tsp	Baking soda
2 tsp	Baking powder

1) Skin, seed and chop oranges. Put into a small saucepan with liqueurs, simmer covered for a few minutes.
2) Meanwhile beat egg replacer with soy yogurt till thick and foamy, then add rest of wet ingredients.
3) Sift together dry items then fold into wet, add oranges (strain slightly first).
4) Spoon into an oiled*round casserole dish (approx. 9″ diameter) bake at 375° for 40 minutes, or until knife comes out clean.
5) Let cool, then turn over to remove from dish. Slice into 2 cakes (horizontally) and frost in between and on top, refrigerate.

Garnish with thinly sliced oranges and raspberries. Serves 4 generously.

*Oil your baking pans by putting a bit of safflower oil or soy margarine on a paper towel and wipe the insides of the pan with it.

Tofu Orange Creme Frosting

Heavenly frosting, chill to set.

5 oz	Silken tofu
2 Tbl	Honey
2 Tbl	Frozen O.J. concentrated
	Dash of cinnamon and vanilla extract

1) Blend till smooth.
2) Refrigerate frosting.

Pineapple Walnut Upside Down Cake

No oil in this cake, yet so moist and delicious!

5	Pineapple rings
1 Tbl	Egg replacer mixed with 4 Tbl water
1 1/2 c	Fructose or natural sweetner
2 c	Wholewheat pastry flour
2 tsp	Baking powder
1 tsp	Vanilla
1 c	Walnuts, coarsely chopped
1 c	Pineapple, crushed

1) Arrange pineapple slices in a circle, on the bottom of a well oiled bundt pan or cake pan of choice.
2) Blend egg replacer, add fructose, flour, vanilla and baking powder.
3) Fold in walnuts and crushed pineapple, pour into cake pan and bake, 350° for 40-45 minutes.
4) Invert when cool.

Serve with **Sauce of Angels** *or* **Tofu Orange Creme Frosting.**

Apple Pecan Cake

A moist cake, not too sweet, great with vanilla soy ice cream.

1 1/2 c	Flour—unbleached
1/2 c	Bran
1 tsp	Baking powder
1/2 tsp	Soda
1/2 tsp	Cinnamon
2 Tbl	Poppy seeds
2	Apples
3/4 c	Pecans—toasted
1/2 c	Soy yogurt
2 Tbl	Egg replacer mixed with 4 Tbl water
1/2 c	Honey or apple concentrate
1 tsp	Vanilla

1) Blend dry ingredients (1st six items).
2) Chop apples, chop pecans.
3) Blend wet ingredients (last 4 items).
4) Fold all together, put into lightly oiled small bundt pan or mold. (Putting a few half pecans in circle on bottom of pan first). Bake approximately 30-40 minutes at 350°. Invert before serving.

Serves 4-6 people

Chocolate Almond Cake

This is lightly sweet with a nice nutty texture. Serve with soy ice cream or with the carob frosting listed—

1 c	Almonds (toast lightly until they begin to pop)
3 tsp	Egg replacer mixed with 4 Tbl water
1/2 c	Eggless mayo (tofunaise, soy mayo etc.)
6 Tbl	Cocoa
1/2 c	Maple syrup (pure)
1/2 c	Honey
1 tsp	Baking soda
1 tsp	Vanilla
1 1/4 c	Wholewheat pastry flour, sifted
1/4 c	Soy milk

1) Grind almonds finely (blender or food processor works well).
2) Put egg replacer, mayo, in food processor and blend, add rest of ingredients.
3 Grease and flour cake pan, pour in batter, bake approx. 35 min. at 375° (to test for doneness, insert a knife in center of cake, if it comes out clean, its done).

Serves 4-6

Carob Frosting

A thick and creamy frosting that is non fattening and high in nutrition.

1 (10.5oz) pk	Silken tofu
2 Tbl	Carob powder
2 Tbl	Honey
1/2	Lemon peel, grated
1 Tbl	Protein powder

Blend till creamy, chill before using.

Peanut Butter Cake with Cocoa Frosting

*This will satisfy those peanut butter and
chocolate sweet tooths.*

Cake:

1 1/4 c	Wholewheat pastry flour
1 tsp	Baking powder
1/4 tsp	Soda
1/4 lb	Tofu
1/4 c	Safflower oil
3/4 c	Fructose
1/2 c	Peanut Butter
1/2 Tbl	Vanilla
1/3 c	Water blended with
1 Tbl	Postum or pero

Frosting:

2 Tbl	Vanilla or chocolate soy milk
1 c	Soft tofu
3 Tbl	Cocoa powder
2 Tbl	Protein powder
1 tsp	Vanilla
1/2 c	Fructose
1 Tbl	Peanut butter

1) Sift together flour, baking powder and soda.
2) Blend next 6 wet ingredients separately. Stir wet and dry mixtures together.
3) Oil and flour a cake pan, shake out excess.
4) Pour cake batter into pan and bake for 35 min. at 375°
5) Blend frosting together (refrigerate to set) frost when cool.

Serves 6

Brownies

A rich nutty treat.

1 1/2 Tbl	Egg replacer mixed with 4 Tbl water
1 tsp	Vanilla
1/2 c	Honey
1/4 c	Soy lecithin spread or soy margarine
1/3 c	Cocoa or carob powder
3/4 c	Wholewheat pastry flour
1 tsp	Cinnamon
1 1/4 c	Walnuts chopped , lightly toasted

1) Beat egg replacer and vanilla.
2) Add honey, soya spread, cocoa, flour and spices.
3) Stir in nuts, put into oiled 7″ square pan and bake 25 minutes at 350°.

Serves 9

Open Sesame Balls

Makes 18 sweet candies

1/2 c	Sesame tahini
1/4 c	Date pieces
1 Tbl	Carob powder
2 Tbl	Honey
2 Tbl	Sesame seeds, toasted
2 Tbl	Coconut, shredded

1) Stir first 5 goodies together, form into balls, about 1" diameter.
2) Roll balls in coconut and refrigerate.

Trailblazers

*These are protein packed balls, perfect for hiking
or other all day adventures.*

1 c	Granola
1/4 c	Pumpkin seeds
1/4 c	Sun seeds
1/4 c	Almonds
2 Tbl	Flax seeds
1/4 c	Bee pollen
1/4 c	Peanut butter or tahini
1/4 c	Barley malt syrup*
2 Tbl	Protein powder

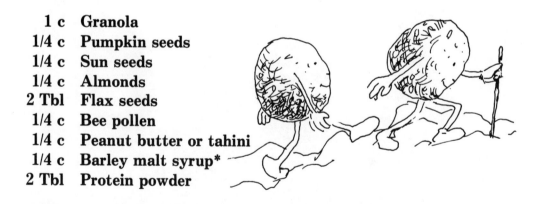

1) Grind granola and nuts until finely ground.
2) Stir in peanut butter, syrup, protein powder and bee pollen.
3) Oil your hands and roll into small balls—chill.

*Add more honey, if necessary, to bind it all together. You can throw
in some dates or raisins too.

Bibliography

Books

Robbins, John. *Diet for a New America.* Stillpoint Publishing, 1987.

Jones, Alex. *Seven Mansions of Color.* DeVorss & Co., 1982.

Kowalchik-Hylton, Claire and William H. *Rodele's Illustrated Encyclopaedia of Herbs.* Rodele Press 1987.

Lau, Benjamin. *Garlic for Health.* 1988.

Erasmus, Udo. *Fats & Oils.* Alive Books, 1986.

Dextreit-Abehsera, Raymond-Michel. *Our Earth Our Cure.* Swan House Publishing Co., 1974.

Kirchmann, John D. *Nutrition Search, Inc. Nutrition Almanac.* McGraw-Hill Book Co., 1975.

Walker, N.W., D. Sci. *Raw Vegetable Juices.* A Pyramid Book, 1976.

Cousens, Gabriel, M.D. *Spiritual Nutrition and the Rainbow Diet.* Cassandra Press, 1986.

Kulvunkas, Victor. *Survival into the 21st Century.* 21st Century Publications, 1975.

Hill, Ray. *Propolis.* Thorsons Publishing, Ltd., 1977.

Wigmore, Anne. *Wheatgrass.* Avery Publishing Group, Inc., 1985.

Burroughs, Stanley. *The Master Cleanser.* Stanley Burroughs, 1976.

References

[1] Erasmus, Udo. *Fats & Oils*. Alive Books, 1986.

[2] Ibid.

[3] Kowalchik-Hylton, Claire and William H. *Rodele's Illustrated Encyclopaedia of Herbs*. Rodele Press 1987.

[4] Walker, N.W., D.Sci. *Raw Vegetable Juices*. Pyramid Books, 1976.

[5] Cousens, Gabriel. *Spiritual Nutrition and the Rainbow Diet*. Cassandra Press, 1986.

[6] Jones, Alex. *Seven Mansions of Color*. DeVorss & Company, 1982.

Alphabetical Index